# RELIGION
## ACROSS
## CULTURES

# RELIGION
# ACROSS
# CULTURES

*A Study in the Communication of
Christian Faith*

# EUGENE A. NIDA

HARPER & ROW, PUBLISHERS
NEW YORK, EVANSTON, AND LONDON

# Contents

# Preface

This volume on *Religion Across Cultures* goes beyond *Customs and Cultures* (1954), which deals with the anthropological context of communication, and beyond *Message and Mission* (1960), which treats primarily the techniques of communication in terms of missionary outreach. I have been concerned here to present more of the psychological and dynamic factors in communication which are universally applicable. This volume also differs rather conspicuously in size from these previous books, for rather than provide extensive documentation or a wide range of illustrative data, the contents of this book have been pared down to the basic essentials, so that the fundamental principles might be more effectively highlighted and the practical implications more readily grasped. At the same time, however, there are a number of bibliographical footnotes referring to significant books and articles dealing with similar or related themes, so that those who seek further confirmation of certain points or who want supplementary information may be helped.

For the manner in which the basic concepts of communication have been treated in this book, I am deeply indebted to my colleagues in the Translations Department of the American Bible Society, and especially to Dr. Charles R. Taber, whose detailed criticisms of content and substantial help in the bibliography and footnotes have been indispensable. My thanks are also due to Miss Dorothy L. Tyler for her critical judgments and editorial assistance.

*Greenwich, Connecticut*                    EUGENE A. NIDA

# RELIGION
# ACROSS
# CULTURES

# 1

# FROM THIRST
# TO BEAUTY

"You may know some of the answers, but you just don't know
the questions young folks are asking," was the reply of a
teenage daughter to her father, a leader in one of the major
denominations of America. This type of response is only too
frequent, for increasingly religion is being treated either like
frosting on the cake of life or psychological padding for the
shocks of human existence. It is either a kind of esthetic
luxury for those who can afford it or a poor man's psychiatry—
where the hard pew is substituted for the soft couch. The
reasons why religious leaders are so largely unfamiliar with the
questions which people are asking today is not merely due
to inattention but to a failure to comprehend the total range
of religious concern. Perhaps, therefore, if we can view religion
in some of its more universal aspects, as religion across cultures, we will be more sensitive and alert to the questions
which are being asked with increasing frequency and almost

frightening urgency by an ever larger group of people in our present world.

## BASIC HUMAN DRIVES

If we are to understand the role of religion in human life, we must examine it in relation to the basic drives and motivations, which are fundamentally the same in all cultures and which are responsible for making all societies "tick." These drives constitute the power and the energy for life, and as such must be distinguished from the so-called "themes" of a culture, that is, those distinctive ways in which a society may express these drives. For example, there is the drive of sex, but it manifests itself in many different forms, e.g., homosexuality and heterosexuality. Within heterosexuality, the dominant pattern involves marriage, structured in terms of either monogamy or polygamy. Polygamy, moreover, may be of two quite different types: simultaneous, as practiced, for example, in many parts of Africa, and serial, the kind for which Hollywood is famous. Heterosexuality may, of course, be expressed outside the marriage relationship with mistresses, callgirls, or prostitutes.

Another basic drive of life is hunger, which some people prefer to satisfy with beefsteak and french fries and others with fried chicken. But many people have radically different ideas about gourmet delicacies. They may insist that boiled snails (France), fried termites (Central Africa), bird's-nest soup (China), raw fish (Japan), or even the half-formed embryo of a baby duck (Philippines) are far superior to bloody beef. Hunger as a basic drive is universal, but the diverse ways in which different societies satisfy hunger—whether in the ordinary food of every day or in exotic delicacies of festal occasions—are the particulars.

What will concern us primarily in this chapter are the universals—the factors which provide the essential base for the over-all view of religion and life.

### THE UNIVERSALITY OF DRIVES

Despite the almost incredible variety of ways in which the different drives of life are manifested, certain of these basic motivations are true of all peoples and all societies. Though, quite naturally, differing degrees of emphasis are placed upon certain drives, and accordingly there are vast variations in values, e.g., the love of beauty versus the desire for food, nevertheless, certain fundamental similarities exist in the response of all peoples to these essential drives or motivations. It is here, if anywhere, that we shall discover the relevance and role of religion.

Sociologists, psychologists, and anthropologists differ as to the number, order, and classification of basic drives. However, there is general agreement as to (1) the distinction between drives and themes, (2) the motivational priority of drives, (3) their universal and indispensable character, and (4) the breadth of human behavior motivated by such drives.[1]

Probably the most basic and immediate human drive is to quench thirst, for life simply cannot long continue without a certain amount of fluid. Moreover, when the body is deprived of it, the sufferer will do almost anything to obtain even the slightest amount. In contrast, hunger is a less immediate drive, for man can go considerably longer without food. However, a minimal amount of food consumption is essential to life, and without it life cannot be sustained.

Sex is also a fundamental drive of life. Not only is its proper expression or sublimation essential to the welfare of individuals, but it is obviously an imperative for the life of the race. However, important as sex is, it does not explain all the essential features of interpersonal relationships, for "to love and to be loved" is no mere epiphenomenon of sexual desires. Rather, this craving for belonging, acceptance, recognition, and love must be regarded as a drive in its own right—as "Primary a phenomenon as sex."[2]

In addition to the drives of thirst, hunger, sex, and belonging, people also exhibit a drive for physical activity, i.e., to move about, to exercise, to engage in physical work and play. Physical activity may seem increasingly anomalous in a push-button, automated society which has gone farther sitting down than any other civilization in the history of the world. But from earliest childhood, the human being displays a craving for a certain amount of physical activity, an essential for physical health and general well-being.[3]

But physical activity is only one phase of man's desire to "do something"; he also has a drive for mental activity. This may mean only scheming how to cheat one's competitors, or it may be devising some brilliant scientific hypothesis; but man was made to use his head, and he insists on doing so. He is also, however, endowed with an important drive for esthetic activity; that is, the desire to experience or create beauty. All societies in one way or another exhibit a sensitivity to esthetic forms, whether painting a picture or only the face or body, the intricate carving of a canoe paddle (Solomon Islands), the complicated geometric decoration of delicate pottery (Eastern Peru), or the polyrhythmic drumming for ecstatic dances (Congo).

### FUNDAMENTAL FEATURES OF HUMAN DRIVES

As indicated in the previous discussion there is a fundamental order in the structured relationships of these various drives, beginning with the most elemental and least dependent and continuing with the most integrated and least independent:

> Esthetic activity
> Mental activity
> Physical activity
> Loving and being loved
> Sex
> Hunger
> Thirst

The twin factors of integration and dependency create a kind of ascending scale: without a minimal intake of liquid life ceases; without sufficient food the activities of life cannot be carried on. Similarly sex is a prerequisite to the continued existence of society and its proper expression or sublimation is a requirement for a satisfactory sense of belonging. At the same time, it will be noticed that failure to establish proper interpersonal relationships largely precludes meaningful physical activity. And without sufficient exercise of the body the activity of the mind is correspondingly impaired. Finally, without thought, esthetic expression degenerates into meaningless forms or senseless blobs of paint.

It will be noticed that no division has been introduced here between biological and psychological drives. Any structured series of such drives tends, of course, toward a set of polar opposites, beginning with the principally biological motivations and leading on to those which are fundamentally psychological. But man is too much of a unit to be neatly compartmentalized into body versus mind. For example, in a number of instances small babies given theoretically adequate formulas in hospitals have been entirely unable to digest their food. Only after they are caressed and loved for thirty minutes or more can they actually digest their food; and in such circumstances they can then thrive on almost any formula. It is a mistake to set a rigid dichotomy between body and mind, between the physical and the psychological, for man is indivisibly one.[4]

There are wide diversities in the ways of expressing basic human drives. Some people may live to eat, while others eat to live. One person may express a completely unselfish, outgoing kind of love, while another will actually commit antisocial violence in order to gain attention. Sex may involve either a beautiful intimacy of selfless giving or a hideous exposure of ego-centered aggression.

Wherever there is serious distortion with respect to any basic drive, the entire life of the individual may be warped out of shape. Children may be so cruelly starved as to suffer irreparable damage to their bodies and minds. Sex perversion may rob people of the capacity for wholesome, interpersonal relationships. The frustration of being deprived of love or minimal recognition may constitute the prime cause of criminal activity.

But when certain drives are not satisfactorily dealt with, i.e., properly expressed or sublimated, a person may seriously regress. Those who have not experienced adequate acceptance by others or have not found some meaning in work, may simply regress to sexual activity, for the sex drive always proves rampant in an existential vacuum. And where the sex drive cannot be properly expressed, some individuals may revert to mere gluttony.

Some people have assumed that each drive exists primarily for itself. That is to say, sex exists for the sake of sex, and mental activity for the sake of the mind. But there is nothing quite so disillusioning as sex for the sake of sex.[5] Furthermore, mental activity which has no goal but activity, results not only in mental inanities but in serious personality distortion and malfunction. Certainly, satisfying hunger is not an activity merely to still hunger pangs, but to nourish the body and thus provide a basis for expressing the totality of existence.

Though some persons have contended that a drive exists for its own sake, many more argue that each drive in turn exists for the ones which are supposedly "higher." Thus ultimately the esthetic drive dominates all the rest, with mental activity coming in a good second. To some extent both were dominant values in ancient Greek society, where truth and beauty were wedded into twin goals of humanism. But sex, belonging, and physical activity should not be thought of as ultimately subordinate to mental and esthetic performance. All drives may be said to be equally justified, but only as the servant of all the other drives, that is, to benefit the totality of life.

### COMPONENTS OF DRIVES

The analysis of human drives and motivations is woefully inadequate unless one recognizes certain essential components in them. Thus, all persons exhibit to some extent a component of aggression in all these drives. This characteristic is likewise spoken of as egocentricity, and in the Scriptures it is described as the way of the "natural man." This means that on each level of drive a person tends to exhibit aggression, whether in the areas of hunger, sex, recognition, or physical activity. Sometimes this egocentricity becomes enlarged and masked as a form of "altruism," and then personal aggression may be hidden beneath the self-righteous cloak of "loyalty" to family, or even of "patriotism" to the State.

To justify the expression of this built-in aggressive component in life, man tends to make himself a god, for he must play the role of deity if he is to be the sole judge of what is good or bad, i.e., good or bad for himself. But man is far too clever to get caught in pure self-worship. He is much more inclined to set up status symbols as substitute idols, for then he can talk about position, recognition, wealth, family, and success, without exposing his excellently contrived masquerade. Ultimately, however, these inflated projections of self are not satisfying. Moreover, when outward circumstances tear away the mask, man discovers to his horror how cheap and futile his life has been.

Egocentricity ultimately becomes a disillusioning experience, for we all know within our heart of hearts that we are not gods and that we are certainly not worth worshipping. Acceptance of Freud's "will to pleasure" as a justification for behavior may lower for the time being our threshold of guilt, but it cannot ultimately satisfy, for it has no lasting significance. Adler's theme of "the will to power," though more nakedly aggressive, is at least more forthright, and within certain contexts probably more sustaining. Viktor Frankl in his plea for "the will to meaning"[6] has been far more insightful. Man must have meaning or his spirit dies before his body succumbs.

It is precisely this craving for meaning which becomes the other basic component of the diverse drives. Moreover, since this component involves meaning which is greater than man, and not merely a rationalized justification for aggression, it stands in continuous and bold contrast to the first component. And because of its transcendental perspective, this component includes the role and function of religion. Man must have ultimates which go beyond self, and it is in these highest "supernatural" sanctions for life that man finds validity in religious expression. Religion is thus not merely one of several basic drives (a capstone of life), but an essential component of all drives, for in religion man seeks the highest and longest lasting good for the totality of existence.

Transcendent meaning usually is expressed in terms of the supernatural, where man seeks to know the will of the gods, the designs of the spirits, and the signs and wonders of the heavens. But ultimate meaning can be expressed in natural terms as well; for example, the order of the universe, or "the will of heaven," as in classical Confucianism. In Communism it is the historical outworking of dialectical materialism, for in classical Marxism this is the ultimate answer to existence. There may be religion without God, and even society without religion, but no society can exist without a reason for being which transcends the structure of the society. A society may not claim to be descended from the gods, but it cannot last for long without charting its course by some ideological star.

### THE AGE-OLD CONFLICT

From the beginning of time the conflict between egocentric aggression and transcendental meaning has constituted man's most fundamental problem. This difficulty, so vividly described by Paul in the seventh chapter of Romans, has always been a crisis element in personal religious life and a "thorn in the flesh" for institutional forms of religion. The clash between such basically antagonistic components has often resulted in cleverly contrived compromises, so as to make life appear rational, agreeable, and even meaningful.

In Buddhism, for example, ultimate meaning is to be found in escape from this world of delusion, and hence by transferring "real meaning" out of the world of people and things, one can more readily make sense out of the anomalies of existence.[7] In Hinduism, aggression, based on ethnic conflict, froze the social structure to the benefit of the ruling castes, but still left some ray of hope for the meaning of life in providing ultimate escape into the world soul of Brahman.[8] Cruelly enough, however, this meaning could be attained only by means of a ritual system completely controlled by the priestly Brahmin caste. In traditional Protestantism personal success and the accumulation of worldly goods have been heralded as meaningful symbols of divine blessing.[9]

In certain instances, aggression has been forthrightly justified by religion. Islam has justified war as a means of ensuring the victory of Allah. The Crusaders were equally proficient in equating the cross of Christ and the hilt of the sword, for in going into battle the priest kissed the crucifix while the warrior kissed his sword. In most instances, however, religious rationalization is far more subtle. One favorite trick is to delude us into thinking that symbolic behavior is more meaningful than actual ethical good. Hence many religionists have taught that real meaning is to be found in ritual performance, for by rites and ceremonies man is supposed to experience truth.[10] Such an approach is always attractive, since talking is so much easier than doing, and acting is so much less demanding than living. Thus, in order to discover transcendental meaning man has frequently elaborated his religious observances in such a demanding manner as to leave little time for much else.

Ritual behavior, however, is not so satisfying to many people as so-called "holy living," for self-righteousness has a tremendous appeal to the small-minded man. As long as the do's and don'ts of religion apply to dietary laws, length of garments, cosmetics, hairdos, and other outward forms, religion is an essentially easy way to appear good; for tithing mint, anise, and cummin is much less difficult than being honest and just. Nevertheless, in the final analysis, self-righteousness cannot be a satisfying experience for the healthy-minded person, for its very focus of attention upon the self imprisons the worshiper within the net of increasingly more intricate and at the same time less relevant rules.

Unfortunately, legalism is sometimes tied to forms of behavior which are not only far removed from religion, but may give rise to serious misunderstanding. In the Cameroun, for example, a man was asked if he were a Christian. His immediate reply was, "Certainly! Can't I read?"; for in his area of West Africa literacy and Christianity were bewilderingly synonymous. In one area of Liberia, in reply to a similar question, an African said, "No, I don't boil water"; for in that particular region the boiling of water was thought to be an indispensable symbol of Christianity.

When neither ritual observance nor self-righteous legalism any longer appeals, the aggressive component of life often deceives people by a subtle form of rationalization which justifies charity "so that you will feel good." That is to say, we are told to do good in order to feel good. The focus of our concern is seemingly taken off self and transferred to another person. But this is only a thin screen for a particularly irksome variety of paternalism, in which self-satisfaction is built upon the hardships of others—a balm only for the truly calloused soul.

## COMPROMISES IN INSTITUTIONAL RELIGIONS

Religions have tended to resolve the tensions between the components of aggression and meaning in three institutionally accepted ways: (1) by shifting attention to intellectual and esthetic forms; (2) by permitting multireligion, and (3) by favoring a syncretistic form of faith.[11]

## INTELLECTUAL AND ESTHETIC ELABORATION
## OF RELIGION

One of the most dramatic illustrations of intellectual and esthetic elaboration of institutional religion is to be found in the history of Buddhism, which found wide acceptance in China during "the time of trouble" at the collapse of the Han dynasty in the fourth century A.D. By offering a plausible explanation for life, a systematic way of dealing with truth, and an impressive tradition of literature and ritual, Buddhism grew with almost incredible speed. Thus by the middle of the ninth century it was the dominant institutional form of religion in China. Its vast monasteries, in which celibacy was practiced, controlled great domains on which peasants worked as slaves to the land. By largely denying the true meaning of sex, robbing the family of its real significance, enforcing poverty upon the masses, and depriving people of a sense of purposeful labor, Buddhism abandoned the central core of basic drives.

In the area of philosophy and the arts, however, Buddhism was remarkably superior. Translations of Buddhist classics were prized and studied by the intellectuals, who elaborated a terminology largely meaningless to the average person. Theological discussions, which had become increasingly abstract and unrelated to life, captured the attention of thousands of monks, who gave themselves unstintingly to the joint themes of discipline and enlightenment. In the esthetic realm as well, Buddhism reached its acme of success. Its embroidered vestments, priceless ceramics, elegantly designed screen paintings, powerful sculpture, and endless ceremonies represented probably the highest development of conscious religious influence upon art forms.[12]

But in another time of trouble, the catastrophic years of A.D. 842–845, institutional Buddhism was swept away by a violent revolution in which Confucianism, with its greater emphasis upon family, sex, work, and belonging, crushed the Buddhist forms, in which these values had become largely irrelevant. The land of the monasteries was redistributed to the poor, and the practical ethics of Confucianism took the place of the largely unintelligible foreign jargon of Buddhist thought.

Buddhism has recently experienced a somewhat similar radical upheaval in Japan. After World War II, Buddhism, previously preoccupied with ritualism and symbolic forms, in considerable measure lost its hold upon people as a way of life. Several sects of Buddhism, however, have arisen during the last thirty years, and except for such common features as the Lotus-sutra, the symbol of the eight-spoked wheel, and a few traditional forms of ritual and ceremony, these new Buddhist sects are quite distinct from traditional Buddhism. Rissho Koseikai, for example, is no elite sect of self-disciplining monks, but a dynamic organization of hundreds of thousands of people who run schools, hospitals, and extensive recreational programs for their members and other interested persons. Soka Gakkai, with its proclaimed ten million members, has been even more successful, but it is certainly not an "otherworldly" sect. The real goals of Soka Gakkai are not Nirvana in the distant future, but personal success in the here and now. To accomplish this goal, forced conversions, political rallies, and good-luck formulas are standard features—a far cry from the doctrines of enlightenment and discipline taught by the Indian saint Gautama, who gave up money and position to be an ascetic "holy man."

Roman Catholicism in Latin America has similarly experienced a tendency toward intellectual and esthetic elaboration. By the time of the Reform in Mexico in the 1860's, fully half the arable land of Mexico belonged to the Roman Catholic Church, with the result that hundreds of thousands of people were essentially serfs of the church. There were massive cathedrals, gilded altars, and awe-inspiring rituals; but except for a minority of the rich who benefited from church-sponsored schools and could afford the costly ceremonies, the church was a master, not a servant of the people. The central core of meaningful motivations lay largely outside the church's concern. During the Reform of the 1860's the church lost its properties; but in league with rich landowners it continued its undisputed control until the Revolution of 1910–1917. At that time the institutional power of Roman Catholicism in Mexico was broken. Gilded altars and fine schools for the elite proved to be poor compensation for the callous disregard of the daily needs of the physically hungry and spiritually impoverished masses.[13]

On the other hand, Protestantism in the United States cannot sit back in smug complacency, for present accusations concerning the irrelevance of the church's message are strikingly applicable to many forms of Protestant worship and practice. For one thing, many Protestants have insisted, and with some real justification, that concern for basic human welfare, involving problems of hunger and housing, are essentially the business of "government agencies." However, many tend to rally behind those political interests which are least interested in doing anything to alleviate suffering and to change the conditions that breed poverty.[14] Problems of sex are often dealt with by a series of "don'ts," and rarely are the basic issues discussed with the frankness with which the Bible deals with sex. This is particularly true in churches with an avowedly conservative orientation. But while a congregation may take false comfort in its strong taboos against dancing, there is often an alarming practice of petting to climax among the youth.[15]

Protestantism has, of course, always had a theology of personal labor; that is to say, work hard, accumulate cash, and become another capitalist.[16] But this is not adequate in our society. The Christian church must also develop a theology of collective labor, and it should be as natural for a Protestant pastor to be chaplain of a labor union as of a service club.

Nevertheless, in the esthetic area of religious expression Protestantism has displayed great energy and concern for tasteful interior decoration, comfortable pews, air conditioning, and well-conducted services, where at least the spirit of the occasion, even if not the Spirit of the Lord, is present. The enormous expenditure on buildings and renovations is only part of the expensive luxury in which Protestantism has been engaged, especially since World War II. One Baptist church in the New York area, whose leadership felt it was impossible to obtain enough money for a full-time director of Christian Education, was nevertheless able to raise over $80,000 for a new organ, remodeled altar, imposing chandeliers, and bright red carpet.

Also in the area of intellectual elaboration, Protestantism has shown remarkable concentration of effort. In considerable measure it has tended to reject the Anglicized Latin in such words as *predestination, sanctification, propitiation, expiation, consecration,* and *conversion,* but has too often adopted such terms as *agape, didache, kerugma,* and *Heilsgeschichte,* which are even less meaningful to the layman. Despite honest attempts by many theologians to reach the secular mind, the average minister seems less and less capable of speaking meaningfully to and about the world and its pressing problems.[17]

Since the growth in church membership in American Protestantism is accompanied by alarming decreases in public and private morality, sociologists have rightly concluded that this form of religion is essentially typical of institutional religion in times of prosperity, when people apparently feel that "glad-handing the Almighty" is good insurance on the way to personal and national success.[18]

## MULTIRELIGION

When a religion abandons certain vital areas of human concern, a kind of ideological vacuum is created which will inevitably be filled in one way or another. Frequently these gaps in a religiously sanctioned value system are supplied by other religions, in circumstances which may be described by the term "multireligion." One of the most striking examples of this phenomenon is to be found in pre-Communist China, where Confucianism, Buddhism, and Taoism staked out complementary claims to the range of interests to which religions speak. This situation can be diagrammatically illustrated, as in Figure 1.

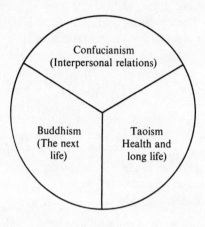

Figure 1

Confucianism, which in general was the religion of the State, provided an explanation for the social structure. Through it men are related to one another, as father to son, mother to daughter, and ruler to people. In this way, men are also related to the past through reverential respect for their ancestors. Buddhism, on the other hand, was concerned basically with an afterlife, not primarily for the group but for the individual, who by enlightenment, self-discipline, and earned merit might ultimately escape from the wheel of existence into the eternal bliss of Nirvana. Taoism concentrated upon the here and now, and by largely magical means promised to help people attain health, long life, and personal success. Thus the three religions combined to cover the total area of man's concern for life, both here and hereafter.

In Japan a similar relationship has existed between Shintoism, Buddhism, and indigenous animistic practices. Shintoism, as the religion of the State, has given meaning to national life and destiny and has related the lower classes to the ruling class, as symbolized by the Emperor. Buddhism has offered man meaning for the next world and tranquillity within the present one. At the same time, animistic practices have always been popular with the common people, who have their good-luck charms and customarily place statues of pregnant bisexual animals in their gardens to promote the fertility of the crops.

### SYNCRETISM

The almost inevitable result of simultaneous religions is a syncretistic form of faith. In eleventh-century China just such an attempt was made to combine Confucianism, Buddhism, and Taoism into a single all-embracing cult. In fact, such syncretism is often accompanied by political overtones, as when Hsien-Chih of Anking, Ahwei, insisted:

> I have examined carefully into the methods of the ancient rulers. When the people are at peace, they have governed and lived according to the proper rules of conduct (Li), but when troubles arise, punishments must be used. When these penalties are not sufficient to control the people, the sanctions of religion must be employed, for men are frightened by spiritual forces which they cannot see nor hear. We know Buddha lived in ancient times. We may employ his teaching with that of Lao-Tsi, even though we do not use their names to reinforce the doctrines of Confucius.[19]

But most religious syncretism is largely spontaneous. For example, in Haiti the elements of West African voodoo religion are combined with Roman Catholic Christianity to produce an amalgam of exotic African rituals and thinly disguised Christian ceremonies. The name of a church near Port-au-Prince is indicative of this syncretism, for it is called "The Pentecostal Methodist National Cathedral of Erzulie." "Pentecostal" denotes its fervor; "Methodist" gives it Protestant status; "National" is meant to suggest importance; "Cathedral" identifies it with Roman Catholicism; and "Erzulie" is a favorite deity in the voodoo pantheon.

In American Christianity, the celebration of Christmas provides an excellent example of syncretism. Even the date of December 25 is derived from the Roman Saturnalia festival season at the winter solstice, and more specifically from the Mithraic feast of *natalis invicti solis* ("birthday of the unconquered sun"). From the ancient Romans comes' the practice of green boughs, while the Druids gave us the custom of hanging mistletoe and the Saxons the use of holly and ivy. The Christmas tree is probably of German origin, perhaps as a functional substitute for the oak, which was sacred to the Teutonic god Odin. Santa Claus is derived from a third-century saint, St. Nicholas, but his toy factory at the North Pole, his reindeer, and his rewarding of good behavior are all more modern myths which exhibit a curious blend of old-fashioned moralism, psychological frustrations, and commercial interests.[20]

TWO-STORIED RELIGION

One special form of syncretism may be conveniently described as "the two-storied religion," for it combines two distinct levels of religious belief and expression. Essentially, the two-storied religion is a compromise between the ideal and the real forms of faith and practice. Ideally, for example, the Christian is a trinitarian, in that he is supposed to believe in one God, consisting of the Father, the Son, and the Holy Spirit. But in reality he is often more accurately described as a polytheist, for he regards these three persons of the Trinity far more as three than as one. Particularly is this true when he assumes differences of motivation within the Trinity by characterizing the Father as stern and harsh while depicting the Son as a kind of culture-hero who reconciles God to the world. The New Testament suggests no such distinction between God and Jesus Christ, but explicitly states that "God was in Christ reconciling the world to himself" (2 Cor. 5:19).

Similarly, Christians are ideally supposed to believe in the brotherhood of man under the fatherhood of God. This should mean that all people are created equal, but for many professing Christians some individuals are evidently judged to be "more equal than others." Hence, in certain respects Protestantism represents one of the most racially conscious and class-oriented major institutions in American life.[21]

God is ideally described as expressing himself in love and judgment, but for many millions of people in America the real symbol of God is not the Father of our Lord Jesus Christ, but a sort of Santa Claus—an indulgent "old man upstairs" who can be cajoled and propitiated by charitable works a few weeks before Christmas (or death!). As one man has said, "This is the best of all possible worlds, for God loves to forgive sinners and I love to sin." This is a god whose arm can be twisted, and who, in many respects, is not much more than a projection of our own secret longings.

One way of justifying a two-storied religion is to insist on certain kinds of religious dichotomies and distinctions. For example, by separating the secular from the sacred, it is possible for some persons to relegate religion strictly to the periphery of life, thus neatly ruling out problems of race, labor, and politics as the concern of the pulpit. "Let the man of God stick to his own business of saving souls" is too often the rallying cry of those who contend that they themselves are quite able to save the world. By making false distinctions between the intellect and the will, or between the mind and the heart, some have thought they could easily compartmentalize their faith and practice. In this way "the world view of the mind" and "the values of the heart" would never come into conflict. With the mind one can then order a world without God, while with the heart one is supposed to find comfort through private devotions. Fortunately this kind of religious schizophrenia is rapidly being exposed in our "secular world."

One favorite "heresy" of some persons is to distinguish between the roles of Jesus Christ. It is claimed, for example, that one can accept him as Saviour, thus guaranteeing eternal salvation, while putting off acknowledging him as Lord until such time as may be more convenient. The Biblical order, however, is not first Saviour and then Lord but precisely the opposite, Lord and Saviour. For the Bible, "Lord and Saviour" are inextricably and inseparably one.

In general, however, people prefer divided rather than integrated truth, for if truth is solidly one, it is likely to prove too demanding. Evidently we imagine that if we can only divide truth, we can rule it; and to rule over good and evil makes us truly gods.[22]

For some persons syncretistic multireligion involves a spreading of religious risks. Thus, the insecure man has a bit of faith in everything, while the more emotionally secure person concludes that there is no need to trust much in anything. Hence, from a condition of believing completely in something, people often slip into a state of believing a little in everything, only at last to believe in nothing. In this way a practical nihilism threatens us with meaninglessness—a condition made increasingly acute as modern philosophy disclaims any desire to provide content or solutions, but seeks only more clever ways of asking more, and more penetrating, questions.

But to understand fully the role of religion in life, we must probe somewhat deeper into the structure of religion and especially into those ways in which man employs its most distinctive feature, namely, its mechanisms for communicating with the supernatural world.

# 2

# FROM GODS
# TO GHOSTS

Religion, since it is so vitally related to the total structure of human personality and behavior, can be studied from a number of different perspectives, e.g., ethical behavior, social participation, systems of belief, and ritual performance. However, communication, a phase of religion often neglected, is one of its most strategic and diagnostic features. For it is precisely in the area of communication that religion differs principally from philosophy, its closest ideological competitor. The philosopher, as well as the religionist, may believe in the supernatural, and may have even constructed an extensive theological structure. The religionist, however, does more than merely believe in the supernatural. What distinguishes him primarily from the philosopher, as philosopher, is that he establishes a communicative link with the "other world" of gods, spirits, and supernatural beings. If we are to understand more fully the cross-cultural implications of religion for human behavior, we must analyze certain significant aspects of religious communication. Not only will such an inquiry give us clues to the way in which religion touches life, it will also provide us with insight into some of the most significant differences between various forms of religious faith.

In this analysis of religion from the communicative standpoint we are not concerned with the "theologized" forms of religious faith, as expounded by the specialists of the various religions. These idealized or "upper-story" forms of Christianity, Buddhism, Hinduism, Shintoism, and Islam show rather striking differences, but life on the "lower stories" of these religions is amazingly similar. For example, the Muslim in West Africa who hangs a juju around his neck, the Mazatec Indian who carries a jaguar claw in his girdle, the Negro who keeps a rabbit's foot in his pocket, and the Christian who thinks a New Testament in his shirt pocket will automatically protect him from enemy bullets are all living on the same plane of lower-story religious expression. Similarly, Japanese who prior to World War II insisted that to be loyal to the nation meant worshipping in Shinto shrines have much in common with many Mexican Roman Catholics, who have declared, *Ser mejicano es ser católico*, "To be a Mexican is to be a Catholic." But some American Protestants are not without similar beliefs. For example, in describing her town a resident of an exclusive Protestant community on the east coast of New Jersey exclaimed: "This is such a wonderful place. Of course, we have no Jews; we have no Roman Catholics; we are all Protestants—we are *so American* here."

## A MODEL FOR THE ANALYSIS OF COMMUNICATION IN RELIGION

If we are to understand the nature of communication in religion, we must employ some kind of model which will help us comprehend the intricate and dynamic relationships involved. Though a model for the explication of a certain set of phenomena may not be entirely adequate, it can, however, help us to understand complex multidimensional structures. In a sense, such a model is only an extended metaphor, but its powers of explanation are so great as to make its use obligatory if we are to comprehend the real significance of religion across cultures.

Two preliminary precautions are necessary in approaching the following discussion. In the first place, no attempt is made to argue the reality of the communication which people think exists between themselves and supernatural beings or powers. If people believe that they engage in such communication, then for them this communication is functionally real. At the same time, Christianity is spoken of in the same terms as any other religion; for it is, of course, one religion among many, even though in certain respects significantly different from others. These distinctive features are treated in a later chapter. Here the communicative elements of Christianity are discussed in a manner parallel to those of all other religious systems.

In contrast to the philosopher, the religionist is one who engages in sending messages to and receiving them from supernatural powers, personal and impersonal. The personal powers

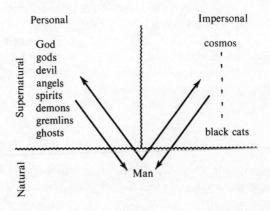

Figure 2

include all kinds of supernatural beings from gods to ghosts—and the impersonal powers dominate the sphere of magic, ranging from astrological forecasts to premonitions produced by black cats. Certain aspects of the communicative relationships involved in such religious communication may be seen in Figure 2.

### COMMUNICATION WITH PERSONAL SUPERNATURAL POWERS

In order to communicate with personal supernatural powers,[1] man sends messages to gods and spirits, largely through prayer, incantations, and special exotic verbal formulas. He may even wish to back up his verbal requests with something more substantial, namely, a sacrifice, which he may perform in order to transmit the essence of his gift into the next world; for just as man cannot pass from this world into the next without dying, so an animal cannot be "sent" into the next world without its being killed. Again, the worshiper may seek some more spectacular way to transmit a gift to the spirit world. Hence he causes it to be totally consumed by fire, since the smoke itself as it rises is presumed to bear the gift to the gods. But communication with the supernatural world is two-way, both sending and receiving, so that the religionist also expects responses in visions, dreams, or verbal revelation, and in such positive benefits as healing and good fortune.

For such communication man normally desires a favorable *quid pro quo*, which will guarantee that he gets more than he gives. This he can do by means of a symbolic exchange, which costs him very little—wads of cheap, make-believe temple money to be burned, or inexpensive effigies to be sacrificed. Some Christians speak about their tithing as "doing business with God," for they insist that for 10 per cent of one's profits one can guarantee success by thus "taking God into partnership." With such a motivation the Christian may become thoroughly paganized.

## COMMUNICATION WITH IMPERSONAL
### SUPERNATURAL POWERS

Communicating with personal supernatural powers seems quite understandable, for these beings are presumably able to listen to what is said, to understand the message, and to decide when and how to answer. Communicating with the impersonal supernatural world is a more complex but common kind of operation, for it is the worldwide realm of magic.[2]

When a Tarascan Indian in Cheran wishes to curse his enemy with ulcers, he must first purchase oil for a lamp, which he then burns for several days before the image of a saint, who is not invoked, but whose presence adds a religious dimension to the deed. He then takes a bit of soil on which his enemy has walked, or a piece of his garment, a lock of his hair, or any substance which has touched his body. As he burns this material over the lamp, he mutters, "In this way an ulcer will come upon your body." Finally, after having drunk some whisky mixed with certain herbs, he believes he has succeeded in cursing his enemy and causing him to have ulcers. In this performance he has not called upon any of the spirits to cause the man harm. He has actually only been manipulating impersonal powers through well-established forms of ritual which have strength in and of themselves.

If a victim wishes to escape the dire consequences of a curse, he must go to some "healer" who is reputed to have even greater spirit power than the sorcerer and who can hence perform white magic for the benefit of the sufferer. The words of white magic can thus "jam the message" of the first curse; for, by having a more powerful message, the healer can negate the effects of the malevolent magic.

The forms of magic are almost unlimited. The Picalqui Indian of Ecuador accomplishes healing by sucking the blood from the leg of a small bird regarded as having a humanlike face. Similarly, a Choco Indian of Panama may kill his enemy by digging out a footprint and planting in it a poisonous vine, thought to have the power to kill its victim. These communications to impersonal supernatural powers are in no sense dependent upon the action of any spirit being who must interpret the message and provide an answer. Rather, magical rites bear within themselves their own inexorable power.

Communications with the impersonal supernatural world are also two-way operations, for answers are expected from these impersonal powers. Horoscopes and crystal balls are thought to foretell the future, while ouija boards, tea leaves, and lines on the palm of the hand are supposed to be sure guides to impending events. The extent to which communications from the impersonal supernatural world are believed in is almost incredible. For example, it is estimated that over 30 per cent of the people of France believe in and consult horoscopes and clairvoyants. Probably a roughly similar percentage of Americans do so. Certainly it is difficult for a society as a whole to claim an advanced "scientific outlook" when most hotels have no thirteenth floor and many airplanes have no thirteenth row.

### THE PERSONAL AND IMPERSONAL POWERS

In Figure 2 the line between personal and impersonal powers is purposely a wavy one, for the relationships are imprecise. The gods, for example, may reveal to men the magic formulas. Moreover, some of these same magic formulas may be used to try to compel God to act on one's behalf. In Haiti, the Psalms are regarded as revelations from God, but this belief also enhances the use of the imprecatory Psalms, shouted at the top of the voice, as the most efficient means of cursing one's enemies. In some societies men may even pray to the spirits in order to have power with magic, while in many areas of West Africa the benevolent spirits have been invoked to keep black magic under control.

The use of magic to control the spirits is particularly important in some religions. For example, a Choco Indian who is trying to heal a sick person must make a hoop of bamboo, then by magical incantations and rites gather on the hoop all the malignant spirits that have caused the illness. Finally, with curses and magic words, he sends the evil spirits off into the darkness.

### THE SUPERNATURAL AND THE NATURAL [3]

The relationship and distinctions between the natural and the supernatural worlds in different cultures are sometimes so difficult to define that some have despaired of doing so. Nevertheless, in all societies the differences between the two are fairly definite. The problem is that the distinctive features differ so widely from one religion to another. For example, among the Anuak people of the Sudan, *jwok*, which refers to all that is supernatural, includes the creator God, the evil spirits, family shrines, groves of trees which are normally avoided, medicine men, any white man (because of his presumed superior control over natural phenomena), radios, cars, airplanes, anything startling, and fate itself. From our point of view, several of these features would scarcely be called supernatural, but to the Anuak they all fit neatly into the same category of the inexplicable world of spirit power.

Nevertheless, the line between the supernatural and the natural, purposely wavy in Figure 2, symbolizes the "coming and going" between the two worlds—indispensable features of many religions. For example, a man at death may become a ghost or even a demigod, while the souls of the dead may return to this world, sometimes to be reincarnated in human form. A person may be possessed by demons, or he may "corral demons" to serve his purposes. Among the Shiriana Indians of northern Brazil, success as a medicine man is dependent upon the number of *hekura* (supernatural spirits) which the medicine man has at his beck and call, most of which are supposed to dwell within him.

### MORAL VERSUS AMORAL POWERS

Most personal supernatural powers are involved in making "moral" decisions. That is to say they must decide whether to respond positively or negatively to the request of the suppliant, whose plea is judged as being either ritually or morally justified, or unjustified. Impersonal supernatural powers, however, are usually completely amoral. That is to say, these powers are neither good nor bad, for not having personality they cannot be judged on the basis of such categories. Often the same ritual addressed to these powers may be used to benefit one man and to curse another. Only in a few instances does magic take on moral overtones. Among the Hehe in Tanzania, for example, one must be very careful about the use of curses to right wrongs; for if magic formulas are employed against an innocent person, the curse will come back upon the individual who pronounces it. Thus even magic may have a kind of built-in morality.

It is significant that those spirits which are thought to be closest to man are normally regarded as the most malevolent or maliciously unpredictable in their behavior. By way of contrast, the spirits more remote from man are conceived of as being generally good. Thus men instinctively attempt to explain the evil in the world, and why, in the midst of the general benevolence of the universe, evil strikes mankind in unpredictable and malicious ways.[4]

### THE USE OF INTERMEDIARIES

Almost without exception intermediaries are used in communicating with supernatural beings. Such go-betweens seem to be both psychologically close to man and spiritually close to supernatural beings. Perhaps this choice of human intermediaries is a response to man's feeling that the gods will be more indulgent when approached by a saint or a spiritual ambassador with a reputation for holiness. A more realistic interpretation may be derived from man's apparent desire to screen himself from the gods. Furthermore, it is convenient to have one-way rather than two-way communication, for the intermediary simply passes on information to the higher power, and since the intermediary knows nothing more than what he has been told, he is scarcely in a position to embarrass the original petitioner by impertinent inquiries or by saying too much. Moreover, in this way the gods are barred, so to speak, from asking embarrassing questions, for their only source of information is the faithful intermediary.

## COMMUNICATION WITH SUBHUMAN POWERS

Figure 2 is in one sense inadequate. That is, it does not represent the total framework of communication in most religious

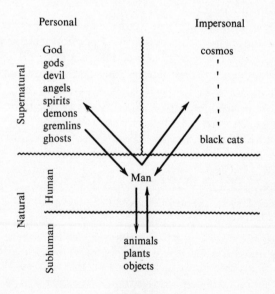

Figure 3

systems, since man also communicates to and receives communications from the so-called subhuman powers. This fuller relationship is diagrammed in Figure 3.

To some extent the subhuman world is also part of the supernatural world. For in many religions all phenomena, including animals, plants, and strange objects, possess some of the soul-stuff which constitutes the mysterious power shared by supernatural and natural beings. Furthermore, not all mankind regards all animals as subhuman. In Hinduism, for example, a sacred cow is regarded as almost divine, and a Brahmin may pray to be reincarnated as a cow.[5]

Communication with this subhuman world may take a number of different forms, including the complex patterns of association with totemic animals. For instance, a Shilluk in the Sudan would never think of killing an animal representing the mythological ancestor of his clan. To do so would not only be sacrilege; it would bring certain destruction. For totemic animals must be respected at all costs, and upon occasion addressed in prayer as with petitions to guide to big game or to aid in gambling.

Communications may also be received from this subhuman world. One may, for example, foretell the future by observing how an animal dies, examining the entrails of chickens, or cracking a caribou's shoulder blade over a hot fire. Or one may gaze into precious stones or crystal balls to foresee the future.

The line between the human and the subhuman world is likewise a tenuous one. According to the traditions of some religions, animals have become men and men may turn themselves into animals. In Tanzania in 1963 a woman was accused of turning herself into a lion and killing a person. She readily admitted her guilt, and so the court had to decide whether, while she was in the state of being a lion, she was still responsible for what she had done. The assumption that the woman had turned herself into a lion was never questioned.

The subhuman world also plays an important part in providing man with symbols for the supernatural world. So elusive

are the gods and spirits that some kind of concrete symboliza-
tion is required for them. Often these symbols are found in
the subhuman world. The Kakas of the Cameroun speak of
God as Njambie, "Spider," while other peoples liken him to a
lion, a jaguar, or even a praying mantis. Sometimes it is not
the individual gods who are symbolized by animals, but, rather,
certain important religious functions are symbolized by them.
For example, the snake becomes a symbol of life and death;
the pig, of fertility; the goat and rooster, of sexual potency;
and the jaguar, of intelligence and death—of intelligence,
because his body is full of eyes; of death, because of the sud-
denness of his attacks at night.

Man's symbols from the subhuman world become even more
powerful when he changes them into idols; that is to say, when
he reads into such symbols more power than he originally gave
them. Such symbols then become not mere representations
of the gods; they *are* gods. The subhuman is then no longer
below man, but around him and above him.

### REASONS FOR COMMUNICATION IN RELIGION

The natural and supernatural world which surrounds man
seems to be completely alive, and as such to be endowed with
incredible power.[6] Otherwise, many events could not be explained, nor would the world make sense. When a tree falls
upon a murderer, the event can scarcely be regarded as mere
coincidence. When, in a testing ordeal, an innocent man
plunges his hand into boiling oil to pick up a small stone at
the bottom of a pot and suffers no burns, surely, it is thought,
this must be more than ordinary cause and effect. When, as
in the northerly flight of the gray hornbill over the bush in
West Africa, the flight of certain birds always precedes the
coming of the rainy season, it is thought that there must be
some relationship between the physical world and the powers
of earth and sky. The Lengua Indians in Paraguay, for example, believe that the rain is brought by birds from the north
that hide behind the clouds, and may not dump their burden

of moisture upon the earth unless they are properly propitiated by the medicine man.

It is natural that man should want to establish some kind of communicative relationship with this strange world of cause and effect, so that he may adjust to its seemingly unpredictable ways. Accordingly it is quite understandable that anthropologists have emphasized man's need for adjustment to the world by means of religious communication designed to establish proper relations with the spirit world. Religion, however, is far more than adjustment to the world; it is also power over that world.

In most instances man looks upon society as consisting of a kind of pyramid, with a few people at the top and many at the bottom. To preserve and justify such a structure, religion serves an important function, for it extends help to the devotee so that he may rise within this structure by the power which

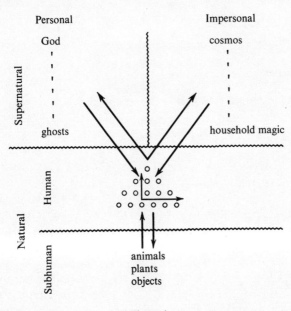

Figure 4

comes from religious observances and magical rites. Religion is thus a source of power, happiness, and prosperity. Furthermore, it provides a technique for extending this power and prestige in time, for it guarantees not only long life, but usually promises future rewards and blessings. For the most part, however, upper-class devotees of religions have emphasized success and power in this world, while encouraging the lower classes to be content with blessings in the future—the "pie in the sky by-and-by."

If we are to diagram religious communications in their broadest scope, we must symbolize this use of religion by man within the social structure as in Figure 4.

# 3

# FROM HINDUISM
# TO CHRISTIANITY

In order to understand the communicative function of religion, it is important to compare some of the principal religions of the world. In this way one may note how religious communication functions within seemingly diverse, but basically similar structures. There is always a danger in any comparison of religions, for in such a comparison there is a tendency to overemphasize both similarities and contrasts. Moreover, in our analysis we are not concerned with the ideal form of the respective religions, but with the "real" form, that is, the manner in which the average worshiper views and responds to his own religious system.

In order to make a meaningful comparison of these major religions, it is essential to employ certain models which will highlight significant similarities and contrasts. Such models inevitably involve problems of representation and interpretation, but despite the inherent difficulties the value of such models is so great as not only to justify their use but to make them almost indispensable. Quite naturally, in any such analysis it is necessary to overlook certain minor differences in order to concentrate on the more essential and diagnostic features.

### HINDUISM[1]

No religion in the history of the world has had so many diverse forms and local varieties of expression as Hinduism, which might be spoken of as the syncretistic religion par excellence. Throughout its history Hinduism has been able to incorporate various deities and thousands of local traditions, but despite such

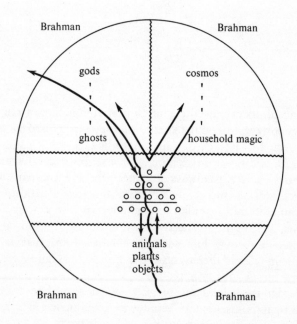

Figure 5

incredible diversity, it has nevertheless maintained certain essential features which make it distinctive. These characteristics may be described on the basis of Figure 5. (As will be noted, this figure closely parallels Figure 4, representing basic communication in religions.)

Within the structure of Hinduism, ultimate reality consists of "spirit," designated generally as Brahman. The physical universe is itself not real, but consists merely of phenomenal manifestations, including everything from gods to things. The supernatural realm consists, first, of the personal supernatural powers, ranging from thousands of gods through myriads of spirits, down to demons and ghosts. Magic is also a very important phase of Hindu religion, though it may be formally disowned by some. However, the influence of the cosmos upon life is regarded as highly significant, and the common man practices many forms of household magic.

Man himself is highly structured into four major castes, and these castes in turn are subdivided into scores of minor groupings. In addition there are the outcastes, those who are religiously and socially banned through loss of ritual acceptability. Within the hierarchy of human life an individual cannot change his social and religious status during his lifetime. By means of ritual purity, however, he can so prepare himself as to be reborn into a higher status.

In Hinduism man's link with the subhuman world is rather close; for failure to preserve ritual purity may result in a person's being reincarnated as an animal, or even in a lesser order of existence. Hence, there is extreme reluctance to kill animals, and certain animals gain almost divine status.

Most of the features of communication characteristic of other religions also apply in Hinduism. Thus there is communication to and from the personal, impersonal, and subhuman worlds. However, one indispensable element in this communicative structure is the Brahmin caste, which is religiously and socially the pre-eminent caste in Hindu society. With only few exceptions ritual purification must be carried out through the mediation of Brahmins, and thus all men are dependent upon the ministrations of this priestly caste to gain salvation and ultimately to be reabsorbed into the great world soul.

Such salvation is, however, essentially an escape from the differentiated physical world (the "real world" of Western philosophy) into the world of undifferentiated .spirit. The escape itself is usually thought to be the result of hundreds, and even thousands, of reincarnations. Finally, by passing through the Brahmin caste, the Hindu may become a demigod, and at last a part of the world soul. In some situations a Hindu may feel that he is privileged to be reborn as a sacred cow, another important step on the path to the spirit world, and ultimately to Brahman.

The keys to traditional Hinduism are ritual purification and Brahmin ministrations. At present, traditional Hinduism is undergoing radical changes, owing to the economic and social revolution in India. Through this revolution caste lines are to some extent breaking down, and old interpretations of religion are giving way to new, demythologized ones. The impact of scientific investigation, even on many of the common people, has cast serious doubt on the escapades of the gods, and the religious monopoly of the Brahmin caste is being not only questioned, but seriously challenged. Nevertheless, for the masses Hinduism is the one hope of final salvation from the struggle of existence; for if man can only keep himself ritually pure, he can finally be reabsorbed into the undifferentiated world soul of ultimate reality.

### BUDDHISM[2]

Buddhism began as a religious protest against the idolatry of Hinduism. Gautama saw no hope in the endless ritual of the Brahmin priests, who dominated their caste-bound society. Rather, he offered to the people a new way of salvation through enlightenment (literally, Buddha) and self-discipline.

Certain essential features of Buddhism, as contrasted with

Hinduism, and as related to the communicative structure of religion, are shown in Figure 6.

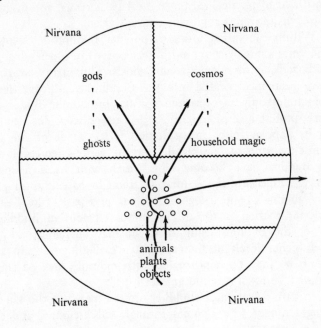

Figure 6

It should be noted that in Buddhism ultimate reality is not Brahman, but Nirvana, often translated as "nothingness." Nirvana, however, is not nothingness. It can be more appropriately described as "zero," for zero is not nothing, but "significant absence of something." From the Western point of view, Nirvana may be said to function as zero, for it contrasts with the phenomenal world. From the Buddhist point of view, however, Nirvana has no such empty quality as zero suggests, for, in contrast with the delusion of physical existence, Nirvana is a state of complete and final bliss.

In Buddhism the physical world is regarded essentially as a

delusion, and thus ultimate reality must consist in the complete opposite of this delusion of physical existence. Accordingly, the antithesis of physical existence must be Nirvana, and to escape into Nirvana must represent true salvation.

Within the varied forms of popular Buddhism, essentially the same kinds of communication occur as in other religions—with gods, spirits, demons, and ghosts. Thus many local gods have been incorporated into the Buddhist pantheon, though sometimes only as capricious spirits. But despite Buddhism's early protest against idolatry, it has nevertheless incorporated in its popular forms many deities. It has made of Gautama himself a kind of "multigod," for the various representations of Buddha have become idols,[3] each with its own special powers, especially if the image is thought to contain a piece of Gautama's bone, a lock of his hair, or a part of his flesh.

Reincarnation is also an important element in Buddhism, for as the Buddhist gains merit he may be reincarnated on ever higher levels of human existence. Failing to gain such merit, he may be reincarnated with radically lowered status, or even be reborn in the animal world.

To gain salvation, a Buddhist must experience the kind of enlightenment which comes through self-discipline, and thus escape from this world of delusion into the pure bliss of Nirvana. He can, however, leave this world from any level of human existence, and is thus not dependent upon a priestly caste or upon being a member of the highest order of society. Moreover, in several forms of Buddhism he may put his trust in a Buddhist savior—some great Buddhist saint who has refused to go out into Nirvana until he can take his disciples with him. Thus the Buddhist savior stands on the edge of Nirvana in order to help his followers escape from the world of delusion into the bliss of nothingness.

Buddhist self-discipline may take many forms, e.g., the life of the warrior priests in traditional Japan or the ascetic practices of Zen, but the ultimate objective of such discipline is to overcome desire. For desire, compounded with ignorance, was regarded by Gautama as being responsible for all men's ills. Hence, only discipline and enlightenment make possible man's escape from delusion.

The religious structure of Islam seems far more intelligible to the Westerner than do Hinduism and Buddhism, because Islam itself has its roots deeply within the Judeo-Christian tradition. In fact, it may be said that in large measure Islam was a socio-religious protest against the dogmatism and corruption of a lifeless, medieval form of Christianity.

Certain essential features of Islam are shown in Figure 7, which describes the communicative relationships among the various essential elements of Islamic faith.

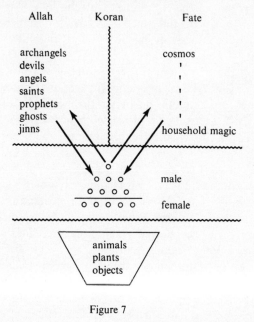

Figure 7

Certain features of Figure 7 provide some significant contrasts with other religions and highlight as well certain internal problems. In the first place, in popular Islam the relative positions of Allah, the Koran, and Fate have never been resolved. It is officially heresy in Islam to suggest that Mohammed wrote the Koran. What he received was simply a copy of something that already existed in heaven. In fact, this was the eternal Koran, which Allah himself is committed to consult. Fate, though essentially the will of Allah, in actual practice is not the desire of the merciful Allah, but a kind of blind chance which even seems to bind Allah's hands.

Beneath Allah there is a whole series of spirit beings, from archangels to the jinns (the genii of Near East fables). These spirits are very real in popular Islam, and in many instances are regarded as more important goals of communication than Allah himself.

Magic is one of the techniques whereby Fate may be either foretold or escaped, and since Fate itself is impersonal, the impersonal techniques of magic seem fitting instruments to control it.

In Islam the two essential religious divisions consist of males and females. For Islam is essentially a male-oriented religion, and women are certainly no better than second-class religious citizens. In fact, women's presence in heaven is regarded in popular Islam as primarily for the sake of men, not for their own sake.

Though in certain syncretized forms of Islam there is considerable communication with the subhuman world (for example, in areas of West Africa), in general the Muslim looks upon the subhuman world as one to be exploited for the sake of man, and therefore his communicative links with it are poorly developed or nonexistent.

Salvation in Islam comes through submission; in fact "submission" is precisely what Islam means in Arabic. Those who submit themselves to the will of Allah may be assured of his protection and ultimate victory. For this reason Islam cannot conceive of Allah permitting the prophet Isa (Jesus) to be crucified, for how could Allah accept the defeat of his prophet Isa? Moreover, Allah himself cannot love to the point of suffering, for though he may be merciful as a sovereign lord or king, he cannot enter into the sufferings of his people to the point of incarnation.

A further aspect of salvation in Islam is to be found in the activities of the people of Allah, who, by the social solidarity of the believing community, are able to join in enforcing the will of Allah, whether by social, political, or military means.


## CHRISTIANITY

Great differences in forms of religious behavior are found in all religions. Hindu practices in the fertility temples of South India are very different from the reinterpretations of Hindu thought proposed by Radhakrishnan. The pictures of cruel torment in the flames of hell which decorate the walls of the Golden Pagoda in Rangoon are startlingly different from the severe simplicity of Zen worship in Japan. The whirling dervishes brandishing swords and crying their allegiance seem quite incompatible with a religion which also includes the mystic Shiites of Persia.

Christianity offers no exception to this diversity in religious expression. The noisy ecstasy of Pentecostal tongues is far removed from the stately ceremonies in St. Peter's in Rome; while the ornately decorated and relic-filled Church of the Resurrection in Jerusalem would seem to belong to a completely different religion from the severely plain, white New England chapel. Nevertheless, certain features of Christianity give it an essential unity, despite many diversities. Some of these elements are represented in Figure 8.

Popular Christianity normally conceives of Deity as consisting of God, Jesus Christ, and the Holy Spirit, in a descending order of importance, and certainly far more in terms of three separate personalities than of a single God. The position of Mary with respect to the three persons of the Trinity is a problem for some Christians. Emotionally, at least, she is sometimes regarded as elevated above God; for is she not revered by some as "the Mother of God"? For others she may act as

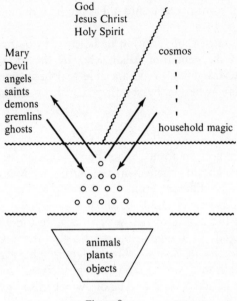

Figure 8

a mediator between Jesus Christ and God, since she seems to be an appropriate mother symbol to obtain favors from a harsh, stern God. For other Christians she holds a position somewhat below that of the Holy Spirit, with varying degrees of isolation and separation.

The reasons for elevating Mary to the position she now occupies in certain branches of Christianity are quite understandable; it is a matter of a built-in psychological necessity. Since God has been depicted so largely as the stern father figure, and Jesus Christ as a symbol of death, it is psychologically imperative that some figure be found to express beauty and life. No one can identify indefinitely with either a symbol of harsh authority or a figure of death. The Holy Spirit, often depicted as a faceless nonentity or an innocuous dove, has rarely seemed capable of fulfilling this positive function.

Accordingly the cult of Mary represents a natural and predictable psychological adjustment.[5]

The role of the devil is ambivalent in many forms of Christianity. Sometimes he has been made almost coequal with God, particularly among those who have wanted to blame him for everything that goes wrong. But for others the devil has been little more than a bogeyman.

The saints constitute an important psychological element in religious communication in certain forms of Christianity, since they provide communicative links with the supernatural. In general they function as one-way communicators and thus provide convenient messengers who carry requests to God but are not too concerned about revealing unwanted additional information to the Deity.

It might seem that beliefs in demons, ghosts, and even gremlins would be seriously affected as a result of contemporary scientific developments. However, gremlins seem to have enjoyed a rebirth as mechanical demons, and interest in communication with the ghosts of the dead has revived, either as a result of widespread interest in spiritism or of a growing faith in extrasensory perception.

Traditionally, belief in influence of the stars on human life (as represented by horoscope readings) has been marginal to Christian faith. Nevertheless, a rapid increase of interest in astrology in western Europe and the United States indicates that it is still important to many. As for household magic, it seems never to have lost its hold upon the masses of people. Faith in the power of lucky pennies, charms, amulets and protective pendants, to say nothing of images, has certainly not diminished significantly in Christendom.

It is, of course, possible to argue that those who hold such presumably nonorthodox views are really not Christians at all. However, it is not our purpose here to judge whether or not these persons are genuine Christians, but rather to describe and analyze the behavior of those who regard themselves as Christians. Some may think such an analysis manifestly unfair, since it seems to put together both the genuine and the counterfeit. However, just as the violent deeds of a dervish mob reflect certain elements in Islam, so the brutal acts of the Ku Klux Klan represent something of fanaticism in Christendom. Both the dervishes and the KKK are parts of their respective systems; and if we are to understand the "lower story" of religious behavior, we must see the totality of religious expression, particularly as it is related to the structure of communication.

In Figure 8 the wavy line between man and the subhuman world is broken, while the animals and objects of the subhuman world are grouped together, as they are in the case of Islam. The broken line identifies the emerging belief among many Christians that man is, after all, some kind of an animal. In fact, many Christians are coming to regard man as biologically and even psychologically quite close to the subhuman world. Nevertheless, for most Christians the subhuman world remains an area for human exploitation of nature, and consequently suffers the ravages of an unbalanced environment, from which he will no doubt continue to suffer more and more.

However, modern Christianity is in a state of rapid transition, so that no one single diagram could reflect all that is happening in the revolutionary upheaval of belief and religious practice. For example, belief in a triune God or Being uniquely responsible for the world in which we live is rapidly losing its hold. Ideally, of course, people in the Western world claim to believe in God, but it is unlikely that more than 20 per cent of those who regard themselves as Christians actually order their lives on the basis of a belief in a supernatural creator, judge, and redeemer of mankind.[6] The scientific revolution of our day has seemed to eliminate God and to have put "scientism" in His place.[7] One would think, of course, that a spread of scientific knowledge would first eliminate the gremlins, demons, and ghosts, for these seem to have less status than God in the supernatural world. Actually, however, it is God Himself who has been made to seem unnecessary and irrelevant, while belief in lesser spirits often continues.

A conversation the author had with an economist, working

for the United States Government on a survey of economic life on Taiwan, may serve to illustrate this significant development in contemporary American life. This man, an elder in one of the leading churches in the San Francisco area, readily confessed that, as the result of his education and experience, he could no longer accept the idea of a personal God or of a unique Son of God, or of the personality of the Holy Spirit. On the other hand, he related a fascinating account of events which completely convinced him that ghosts are real. A short time before he had bought a house in San Francisco from the estate of a recently deceased woman. This man and his family moved into their new home one afternoon, carefully closed all the doors that night, only to discover that all the doors were unlocked or open the next morning. On the next night precisely the same thing happened. On the third night the new owner, when he heard a slight noise in the living room shortly after retiring, went downstairs, addressed the former owner by name, and assured her that he and his family greatly appreciated the new home in which they were living, and promised that they would give the house the best of care. After this incident the doors were never found open or unlocked in the morning.

This particular experience was of course unique to this person, but it nevertheless typifies the kind of evidence many professing Christians implicitly believe. To many, the traditional God of Christianity seems far away, and quite unconcerned with the affairs of life. In contrast to an ancient and indefinable God, in whom they only vaguely believe, stories about ghosts and communication with the dead seem much more plausible, especially if theories about extrasensory perception add scientific window-dressing to the tales. Accordingly, if we are to represent accurately the beliefs of some persons, Figure 8 should be redrawn, with the line separating spirit beings and the impersonal world shifting from northeast to northwest. Modern pseudo-science would then occupy the place of major deities, but still leave plenty of room for nearby spirits and technological gremlins.

Scientism, as an absolutizing of scientific observations, has actually become a dominant form of faith in the Western world. Unfortunately, many persons confuse description with explanation, and conclude that the descriptions of science have explained the universe without need for God or any non-physical factors. Such "explanations" tend to exalt man at the expense of God, and thus to flatter him even if they cannot satisfy him. Moreover, scientism and its near relative, pseudo-science, have given birth to a distinctive mythology, widely known through the rapidly proliferating field of science fiction. Despite our much vaunted confidence and pride in the publication of scientific reports, it is still a fact that more people read science fiction than science. This type of scientism, however, has not eliminated either the spirits or the belief in impersonal supernatural powers. In Paris alone there are more astrologers than schoolteachers, a telling indictment of the supposed intellectual quality of the Western world.

For some religions salvation may result from ritual purity, enlightenment, and discipline or submission; while in popular Christianity salvation comes first from keeping the Ten Commandments, secondly from trying to follow the Golden Rule, and thirdly from being conscientious about church attendance, with special emphasis in some forms of Christianity upon the efficacy of the sacraments.[8] If the people know anything about "salvation by faith," it is usually in terms of "You can't understand it, so you must have faith"; while authority is interpreted largely as "You've got to believe the priest" or "That's what the Bible says."[9] Increasingly, however, it is regarded as unthinkable that God could possibly condemn to hell anyone except the most vile criminals. Hence to avoid eternal judgment one must not be too bad (everyone is expected to have some pet sins); but above all else one must be conscientious. In fact, so the popular view goes, it does not matter much what one believes so long as one is conscientious in what he believes; for conscientiousness is the religious quality par excellence in the thinking of many people. Of course, there are those who talk about being saved by the blood of Jesus, and in some way or other the death of Christ on the cross is supposed to be related to ultimate salvation;[10] but this is never spelled out very clearly by the average person who thinks of himself as a Christian. In fact, many Christians in the Western world are becoming less and less interested in eternal salvation. They appear to be doing so well on earth without God that heaven seems to offer few rewards, and hell appears to provide little basis for fear.

But if we are to assess properly the role of religions across cultures, we must view them as something more than mere communication systems with the supernatural. Each religion also possesses a dynamic dimension of rapid and radical change which deeply affects the lives of its adherents. This means that we must look at religion from its historical perspective, and in this respect perhaps no religion is so instructive as Christianity, for it has undergone such fundamental changes during the centuries and is now being challenged as never before in its history. These are the important developments treated in Chapter 4, "From Medieval to Modern Man."

# 4

# FROM MEDIEVAL
# TO MODERN MAN

All peoples demand of their religion an explanation and a validation for the structure of their society and the distinctive features of their life. Thus for the ancient Quiches of Guatemala, man could be explained only as the result of a series of attempts to create human life. These attempts finally succeeded, they believed, when the gods made four progenitors out of corn. From these first four men, created from both yellow and white corn, all the clans and tribes on earth descended. These earliest men, however, could see so clearly and understood everything so well that the gods immediately realized they themselves would be challenged by fierce competition from human beings. Therefore, the eyesight of these men had to be limited and their capacities reduced by having mist blown in their eyes. In this way the Quiches tried to explain not only the diversity of peoples but their evident human limitations as well.

To explain the pre-eminence and distinctiveness of the Japanese, the religion of Shinto has claimed direct descent of the Emperor from the sun goddess, Amarerasu-chikami, and genealogical and emotional identification of the Japanese people with the great Kami of the age of the gods.

But all religions seek similar types of validations for their structures and ways of life. Even in Christianity different denominations seek to prove the superiority of their organizational structures by quoting from the New Testament, though obviously in a selective manner, for no single document such as the New Testament could possibly validate all the church organizations which claim to be based on New Testament principles and practices.

### RELIGIOUS VALIDATION OF MEDIEVAL SOCIETY

In the Middle Ages, Christianity was required to provide validation for the structure of life; for religion must offer a means

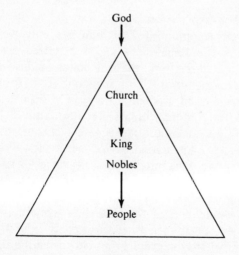

Figure 9

of communicating with the supernatural powers of the universe and also prove that the form of society is essentially in keeping with the requirements of the supernatural powers at all times—past, present, and future. This validation of medieval society is schematically shown in Figure 9.[1]

In the medieval view of the world and society, the authoritative basis for human life was provided by the power of God, as expressed through the Church (and especially through the Pope as the personal representative of Jesus Christ), and then mediated to the people through the king and nobles. Moreover, this supernatural validation of the authoritarian structure gave the Church and the king power over life and death.[2] During this entire period, there were certain conflicts between the secular and the sacred power structures, both in the Church and in society; but for all practical purposes the Church insisted, and the majority of the people agreed, that God relayed His truth and validated His choices through the judgment and action of the Church.

### THE RENAISSANCE

The medieval explanation of how the judgments and power of God were communicated to human society was basically disrupted by the Renaissance and the related event of the Reformation. At this time the real power of the Church was thoroughly undermined.[3] This may not seem to have been true, particularly in Roman Catholicism, since at this very period the Inquisition, with its absolute authority, was instituted. However, an inquisition is a sign, not of strength, but of weakness, for totalitarian devices are evidence of inherent failure in a power structure. A further evidence of the Church's loss of power is the fact that precisely during this same period the doctrine of the divine right of kings became dominant. With the elimination of the Church, supernatural validation for the structure of society passed directly from God to the king, and finally to the people, thus circumventing the Church, as illustrated in Figure 10.

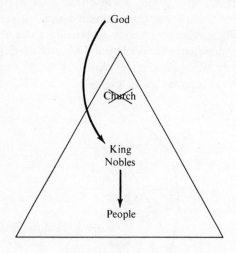

Figure 10

### THE AGE OF REVOLUTION

What may have satisfied Western Christendom for a time during the Renaissance proved to be inadequate for a later time. During the Age of Revolution, primarily in the eighteenth century, the real power of kings was destroyed. Of course, in many societies (for example, Great Britain) the king or queen continues to reign, but not to rule. To all intents and purposes the king as an indispensable mediator of divinely derived power has been largely eliminated from modern society.

Religion was called upon to explain, at least in some measure, the relationship of God to man, and again a convenient formula was found in speaking about man's "God-given inalienable rights." Thus the people themselves, as the essential constituent parts of a society, are provided with divine sanctions for ruling themselves. This early type of "God-inspired" democracy was founded upon a form of humanism with deistic dimensions (especially so in the case of Jeffersonian democracy). With both Church and king eliminated, society was validated by man's personal accountability before God,[4] as represented in Figure 11.

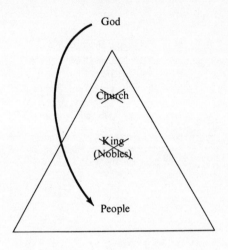

Figure 11

## THE AGE OF SCIENCE

In the Age of Science, God, as defined in traditional formulations, has been largely eliminated from the thinking of those who carry on the affairs of the Western world. Nietzsche was right when he insisted that, for many people, God was dead. But the "demise of God" confronted man with a serious socio-religious trauma; for if God himself has been eliminated, how can man any longer validate his existence and his ways of life? Without the supernatural sanctions which come from God, where is man to find those superhuman categories which will justify his social structure and tell him where he has come from and where he is going?

Bereft of the supernatural sanctions derived from God, man has actually begun looking down to the subhuman level of existence to find authentication and validation for life. Thus, instead of basing human values on a kind of God-given humanism, he has sought to find justification for life and its patterns of existence in an evolutionary naturalism, the main structure of which is represented in Figure 12.

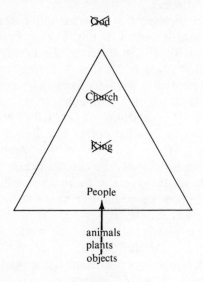

Figure 12

This subhuman world has constituted not only the basis for the explanations of biological evolution but much more importantly, from the standpoint of human behavior, the theories of social and historical evolution.[5] Thus an attempt has been made to supply modern man with an orientation for life. Man is never content simply to exist without a rationale for his life. He must validate the present by his view of the past and fashion today to fit his picture of tomorrow.

Fascism and Communism both expropriated the evolutionary explanation of history[6] as a basis for building their theoretical structures, though interestingly enough in quite different ways. Fascism, for example, has preached the evolutionary development of the superman and the superrace, thus implying that biology itself justified territorial expansion and the realization of a people's historical destiny. As was proved in the decisive events of World War II, there was no such superman or superrace; but the idea of racial superiority does not die so quickly, for Fascist tendencies lie close to the heart of small-minded men.

Communism represents a far more subtle approach to an evolutionary view of human destiny. During its earlier periods Communism in Russia insisted upon the hereditary transmission of acquired characteristics, and in this way sought to reinforce its essentially historical form of evolution by some biological justification. But Communism is not dependent upon biological interpretations, for its "faith" is based on dialectical materialism, growing out of Hegelian views of thesis, antithesis, and synthesis. According to the popular interpretation of Communism, it was the conflict between agriculturist and herdsman which gave rise to ancient civilization. Later the struggle between slaves and free men was thought to have produced Classical society, and in late Medieval and Renaissance times the wars between serfs and nobles were regarded as the basis for the Industrial Revolution. Within our own period, the struggles between labor and capital are thought to lead inevitably to world Communism.

This view of history has a strong appeal, for it implies that creativity rises out of destruction and that conflict gives birth to something nobler and higher. Thus destroying, always easier and more congenial to many than building, provides a powerful incentive to rebels, who can justify evil as a means of creating good. This view involves a serious misreading of history, for it has been, not the violence of the masses, but the action of the creative minorities which has produced significant advances. In saying this, one need not underestimate the importance of revolution in the history of the world, nor minimize the stifling effects of a status quo attitude in a society. Nevertheless, truly creative changes are introduced by builders, not by destroyers. Dialectical materialism, however, has already passed its intellectual zenith—its logical inconsistencies and its practical inadequacies are all fully evident for men to see; but the power of Communism based upon such a theory of society has certainly not passed its military or political peak.

## EXISTENTIALISM

It is not at all strange that Existentialism should have arisen in circumstances in which, for many, God is dead and sub-human forms of life have proved inadequate to explain the uniqueness of man. For Existentialism is precisely a system of looking at truth which refuses to accept the supernatural, at least in its traditional forms, and at the same time insists that the answers of Fascism and Communism are no answers at all, and that man is simply not explicable as merely a quanti-tatively more complicated animal.

Existentialism is not a "content" philosophy, in the sense of a system of truth, but it offers a very important way of looking at truth, since it raises questions in ways which earlier forms of philosophy have not considered. In fact, societies and periods of history are distinguished, not so much by the answers they give to life, but by the questions they ask, and the ways in which they ask them. In this regard Existentialists have sought to pose some relevant questions about man's search for meaning, his freedom, his ambiguous relationships to his fellow man, and his incredible capacity for self-deception.

Existentialism cannot be expected to put God back in the heavens, for a way of examining truth is not a technique for proving the existence of anything. But Existentialism has served a very useful purpose in destroying some age-old idols. For one thing, it has exposed, with heartless cynicism, the idea of the inherent goodness of man by turning the spot-light on man's demonic capacities for evil and self-deception. Existentialists such as Kierkegaard, Jean-Paul Sartre, and Albert Camus have all exposed the moral nakedness of man.

Existentialists, however, have not made man out to be

merely a beast or some highly complex animal, but as qualitatively a different "animal," not only because he is essentially a user of symbols, but also because he lives constantly in the presence of the great Existential question of life and death—something which makes the human being utterly distinct from other animals

Quite understandably, the Existentialist has also refused to look at man as merely a spectator sitting on the sidelines of life; for in the Existential view there are no spectators; all men are actors. Moreover, presumed objectivity is not to be found by the person who isolates himself from the very phenomenon he is studying, but rather by the individual who is immersed in it. This means that the best judge of Christianity is not the outsider, who looks in upon Christian behavior, but the Christian who himself participates in the very activity he wishes to describe. In a sense, of course, it also means that complete objectivity (in the traditional sense of the word) is impossible, for we are all—whether we like it or not—a part of the very life we study and evaluate. It is only that we must be honest and fair.

Probably one of the most significant contributions of Existentialism has been its revolt against the mere intellectualization of life. In fact, Existentialists have been emphatic in their denial of thought as a substitute for action or of words as a substitute for life. Theology is thus not religion, any more than grammar is language.

## THE PREDICAMENT OF MODERN MAN

In the past Western man either has had a religion which would explain to him his origin and destiny or has adhered to a philosophical system which attempted to do so. Philosophy, however, in the form either of Existentialism or of logical analysis (an increasingly dominant element in modern philosophy) has openly rejected this type of goal. Existentialism turns out to be largely a systematic way of asking questions about a systemless universe, and logical analysis has become a method for studying statements *about* reality rather than an investigation of reality itself.

Thus for modern Western man neither religion nor philosophy seems to provide a structured view of society or a validation for a way of life. Man is simply left to sink or swim in a seemingly absurd and systemless world. On the other hand, the physical world which surrounds man seems to be systematically organized and efficiently structured. It is only man himself who appears to drive mankind to intellectual despair. Undoubtedly part of the problem lies in man's failure to comprehend and to respond meaningfully to relevant religious communication.[7]

Relevance in religion is one of the universal problems faced by men and women in all cultures. Some of the present-day developments in Buddhism in Japan are encouraging attempts to face up to the realities of a new world, but perhaps no religion has experienced such new and creative approaches to the threats of a desupernaturalized universe as are now taking place in some of the dynamic movements in Christianity, considered in Chapter 5.

# 5

# FROM MAN
# TO MAN

The communication of Christian faith is to many persons a
completely hopeless task. In the first place, Christianity is
"old stuff," an ancient or medieval view of life which is no
longer relevant in a technological society and a "post-Christian" era. To them "post-Christian" means essentially that
"God is dead," and not merely in the sense that modern man
no longer believes in God. For some radical theologians, not
only is the belief in God dead, but God Himself is nonexistent, and hence belief in Him is not only false but irrelevant. While nineteenth-century rationalists often spoke of a
religion which included God but rejected Jesus Christ, certain
modern theologians would accept Jesus Christ while rejecting
God, thus making Jesus a kind of religious culture-hero. But
if God is dead, obviously Christianity cannot proceed without
"resurrecting" Him. Such a task, however, is ideologically impossible; it is easier to propagate new gods than to revitalize

old ones. Hence, some would argue that the Church may just as well give up.

To make matters worse, the Bible as the authority of the Church seems to have fallen into disrepute, for its prescientific setting seems ill adapted to modern-day communication. Since many have concluded that they cannot believe in Biblical infallibility any more than in papal infallibility, they are ready to scuttle their faith.

A still further aggravating aspect of this problem is the seeming failure of the Church to respond to the challenges of our own day. For, despite courageous efforts on the part of some few individuals, the Church as a whole has not distinguished itself in facing up to controversial issues.[1] What has seemed even more frustrating to the average layman is that many theologians and church leaders are most pessimistic about the future of the Church and the relevance of Christian faith. Hence, for many people, God may as well abdicate and let His ministers go into exile in the secular world.[2]

## BIBLICAL RENEWAL

But despite the alarming pessimism of church leaders and the seeming impotence of the church as an organized institution, the modern world is experiencing a Biblical renewal of unprecedented proportions, not merely in the "new nations" but also in some of the sophisticated centers of the Western world. Even the demand for the Scriptures has grown greatly within the last few years, so that the United Bible Societies almost tripled their circulation in the years 1964–67, reaching a total of about 100 million copies of Bibles, New Testaments, Gospels, and selections.

Despite the claim that the Bible is no longer intelligible to modern man, there are more people reading and studying the Scriptures, whether individually or in small groups, than at any time in the history of Christianity. Even the "revival meeting" has been revived in a number of communities, though not in the traditional form of a ritualistic, yearly catharsis for church members who enjoyed hearing sinners denounced and the blessed commended for their state of grace. The present-day equivalent of the revival meeting is far more closely tied to life, and hence can be far more meaningful.

Though the statistics of failure in church growth are alarming in some areas, there are nevertheless certain regions in which the communication of Christian faith is taking place with refreshing and dynamic relevance. Some of the most spectacular occurrences of Biblical renewal are in those areas where the Christian faith is relatively new, e.g., Indonesia, East Africa, or where the traditional forms of Christianity are so overlaid with pagan accretions as to be scarcely recognizable, e.g., many places in Latin America. For in both of these types of situations new and vital movements have emerged within the last few years, giving promise of considerable growth and dynamic in the future. But the movement of the Spirit of God is by no means restricted to these "missionary areas" of the world. There have been a number of fresh, creative developments in the Western world—instances of genuine renewal of Christian faith, which may constitute the really hopeful signs on the horizon of what is otherwise a bleak landscape.

### THE WORD OF GOD COMES TO THE VALLEY OF TASQUILLO

Some twelve years ago a Texas Mexican, traveling along the International Highway north of Mexico City, shared with Venancio Hernandez his faith in the living God. Don Venancio, an Otomi Indian who was also literate in Spanish, then began to study the Scriptures for himself and to share with his friends this new life which he had found. At first the persecution by local Roman Catholic fanatics was crushing, but gradually a small congregation formed and they began to share their new faith with neighbors and friends throughout the Valley of Tasquillo. Despite further persecution, and ultimately the martyrdom of three of their members, this movement of the Spirit of God now includes more than twenty churches and more than 3,000 members in what is one of the most poverty-stricken and fanatical regions of Mexico.

When asked to explain what had happened in the region of Tasquillo, Don Venancio said, "Oh, we just believe in redemption." And then he described first the "redemption of people's hands." He meant that the Christians in the town of Ixmiquilpan were teaching one another new trades. Don Venancio himself had invented a new technique for making longer and stronger rope and had also improved a loom so that it could be used to knit sweaters both of better quality and more rapidly.

To meet one desperate situation, the church in Ixmiquilpan had itself undertaken, with the help of a government engineer, to build a road into a poverty-stricken valley. The entire congregation would meet Sunday morning at five o'clock to worship, and then the whole day would be given to work on the road, after which the people returned to glorify God. Some members of the congregation, who could spare time during the week from working in the fields or as masons and mechanics, helped on the road, so that actually it was built six months ahead of schedule—perhaps the first time in the history of Mexico that this has happened. Persecution had excommunicated the people from various small towns and villages, but the believers soon banded together, purchased an abandoned hill along the highway, and there built a village of well-constructed homes, which now has electricity and a sewage system. Here the power of the living God has redeemed the work of men's hands, and the whole economic life of the Christian community has been transformed.

For this Christian community, however, redemption also involved "redeeming the head," for every member of the community was under obligation to share with others information about his own trade or skill, such as typing or car mechanics. While old ladies were weaving mats or baskets for sale in the market in Mexico City, a local schoolteacher would be at a blackboard to teach the ABC's. From the youngest to the oldest the whole community became intensely concerned to acquire new skills and knowledge.

This community of believers also believes in the "redemption of the body," in the form of "divine healing." Not only have many of these people been so poor that they could not afford standard medical treatment, but they have insisted that God can and does perform miracles of healing in their midst. The numerous instances of otherwise inexplicable cures are evidence of their faith and confidence in God's power to touch their bodies. Nevertheless, this community has not become fanatical about divine healing, nor has their faith in such healing prevented them from using medicines, or from encouraging some of their members to become nurses, or from putting in a proper drainage and sewage system for the town.

In conclusion, Don Venancio insisted that this community believed in "redemption of our souls," that is to say, of the total person. But it was interesting to note that he first talked of hands, head, body, and then of the soul.

Perhaps one of the most revealing aspects of this movement of God's Spirit is the procedure employed by these Christian leaders in making contacts with other communities. Sometimes people in other areas hear of what has happened among the Evangelicals in Ixmiquilpan, and invite them to visit and tell "what God has done." In other instances the leaders in Ixmiquilpan feel constrained to "witness" to a particular community, especially one which may be fanatically opposed to the Gospel. Before doing so they always spend a weekend in prayer and fasting in the hills above the village in question, where they ask God's power and guidance to direct them in their approach to the people. Then, when they enter the village, they engage the people in conversation, primarily asking them whether they want progress. As Don Venancio explained, "If it is a poor man, he always says he wants progress, but it is the rich people who exploit the poor and therefore no progress can ever be made. If, however, the person is a rich man, he likewise says he want progress, but insists that it is the stupidity and backwardness of the poor which makes progress impossible." Gradually, however, the conversation turns on the theme that progress is possible only when people themselves are changed; and perhaps such a change is necessary if there is to be progress. In this first contact, the only purpose is to obtain a friendly opening, so that others of the congregation may return, especially one of the ranchero-music bands (the congregation in Ixmiquilpan has four such bands). On some appointed day the people come with their bands and music, bringing a soccer ball for sport in the afternoon and colored slides to depict the life of Jesus Christ against some white-washed wall at night. Here is no high-powered pressure program, but a genuine desire on the part of the Christians to share with others the meaning of true "progress."

The worship service in the Ixmiquilpan congregation is likewise indicative of what has happened in this Christian community. Beginning on Sunday evening about five o'clock, people come to the church to pray and to share with one another what God has done for them. Gradually, as more and more people assemble, singing begins about six o'clock, and by six-thirty some of the bands have begun to play. It seems that almost everyone in the congregation plays an instrument, but not everyone owns one, and so instruments are left on the platform and anyone who cares to participate comes and plays. In the midst of one joyous period of singing, the leader may exclaim, *Que siga la fiesta* ("May the festival continue"). For here in the singing and acclamation of joyous experience, people have a "foretaste of heaven itself." About eight o'clock, the leader shouts to the people, "What do we want to hear more than anything else?" to which the congregation exclaims in reply, "To hear the Word of the Lord." At this point the pastor comes forward and leads the people in a study of the Word of God, after which the Lord's Supper is observed. Finally the people leave for their homes, singing, chatting, and sharing with one another the joys of the evening and the new experience which they have found in their lives.

The dominant themes of this congregation are "the love of God" and "the victory which we may have through Jesus Christ"—Biblical realism at its theological best.

One must not, however, think that the experience of the churches in the Valley of Tasquillo is unique. There are four groups of indigenous churches in Mexico; some groups include as many as 400 churches. Though these groups are only about thirty years old, they actually account for about half of all the Evangelicals in the country. In Chile, the indigenous Pentecostal movement is four times the size of all the other Protestant organizations put together, while in Sao Paulo, Brazil, the Pentecostals have laid the foundation for the largest church in the world, to seat 25,000 people.

The power of the Word of God reaches, however, not merely to the Spanish- and Portuguese-speaking people of Latin America, but also to some of the more primitive areas. There are, for example, about 5,000 Curipaco Indians in the southeastern corner of Colombia. Fully 90 per cent of them are now Christians, and almost 95 per cent are literate. Moreover, they have begun to evangelize neighboring tribes, so that at present there are probably some 10,000 Indians whose lives have been vitally affected by this movement of God's Spirit.

Other areas of the world have also been dynamically transformed by the Gospel. In East Africa, a revival which has been going on for some thirty years has had a profound effect upon tens of thousands of people—both Africans and Europeans. With such themes as "the Calvary road," "living in the light as He is in the light," and "life without ceiling and without walls" (that is, nothing to separate the believer from God or from his fellow Christians), it is easy to see how those whose lives have been vitally affected by this revival have themselves been instrumental in providing a basis for real interracial understanding.

Even in the most backward area of the world, where men are only a few years removed from Stone Age cultures, namely, in eastern New Guinea, more than 25 per cent of the indigenous population is associated with Protestant or Roman Catholic churches. Even though some forms of Christian expression are strangely mixed with pagan practices—especially when communities become victims of the cargo cult hysteria—nevertheless, there is a genuine emergence of a dynamic New Guinean leadership, spiritually sensitive and determined to see the power of God expressed in the lives of men.

Even in a place like Indonesia, in the midst of crushing economic circumstances, powerful propaganda pressures, and intense nationalistic demands, Christians nevertheless express a dynamic optimism which would put to shame the "God is dead" theologians. If any churches had reason to give up in despair, certainly the churches of southeast Asia would be justified in doing so. But this is far from being the case. Perhaps only those living with moribund institutions think that God is dead. For those who experience the power of the living God, it is not so.

### THE WORD OF GOD AND MODERN MAN

Many persons argue that it is well and good for primitive or backward peoples to accept the Scriptures, for the Bible fits the primitive, pretechnological societies, while modern, sophisticated man is unable to understand the Bible or even to be interested in it.[3] Such an opinion is, however, radically contradicted by the enormous increase in group Bible study, not merely in Protestantism, as noted above, but in Roman Catholicism, particularly in France, Germany, and now in Latin America and the United States. The *cursillo* movement, begun in Spain a few years ago, and rapidly extended to Latin America and the United States, is a dynamic Roman Catholic program for combining lay witness, intense personal sharing, Bible study, and personal rededication. Even in the Coptic Church of Egypt emphasis upon Bible study has brought vitality to various aspects of the lay movement.

It is quite impossible to cite all the significant contemporary movements which exhibit a dynamic Christian vitality, but some of the more characteristic of these programs in the

United States include: (1) those related directly and indirectly to the publication *Faith at Work*; (2) the Laymen's Leadership Institute; and (3) work among juvenile delinquents, as in Young Life and in the Youth Development Program. A number of other significant programs exist in the United States, Canada, and Europe, but those noted are typical of a new dynamic element in Christian expression.

One of the principal difficulties involved in discussing some of these significant movements is the fact that many do not have typical organizational structures, there are no membership lists, no statistics are kept, and thus there is simply no way of knowing how extensive the movements are, nor of judging their impact. Nevertheless, these and other dynamic, practical expressions of faith may provide the basis for a turning point in modern Christianity.

*Faith at Work*, a magazine published monthly in an edition of approximately 30,000, is sent to individuals and churches all over America, as well as throughout the world. Its presentation is so modern as to be suspect by the stanchly orthodox, and its emphasis upon vital faith is so evangelical as to make it questionable to the liberal left. One number, for example, may describe a concept given by Duke Ellington at Grace Cathedral in San Francisco, where modern music and deep religious conviction were communicated together. Another story deals with a transformation at Fox Lake Prison in Wisconsin, where prisoners are learning to experience the power of God through Bible study and small group sharing. Another article deals with laymen as evangelists, a program being developed in various parts of America, where ministers, together with their laymen, may be said to "conduct revival meetings," usually over a long weekend in a church. The laymen stay in the homes of members of the congregation and share with them and other small groups what God has meant to them. These laymen do not presume to answer all the questions, but they show how men and women have been willing to "test God" in the midst of the everyday experiences of life.

Various conferences under the leadership of *Faith at Work* have as many as 1,000 persons in attendance—people who come together, not to push any particular program or institution, but to find out how to express in everyday experience the power of God.

The Laymen's Leadership Institute is a similar informally organized program which conducts a long weekend institute once a year. To this institute are invited leading business and professional men, not to determine major policies of church or society, but to discuss in small groups and under the leadership of other laymen how Christ can become real in the home, business, society, and church. For example, groups discuss such questions as "Is there such a thing as a Christian business?" "How does one get time to read the Bible?" "What do we really mean by family devotions?" "How can young people be kept from rebelling against too much religion?" No one pretends to have all the answers, and there are no neat formulas spread out for people to analyze, memorize, and apply. But the dynamic of Christian openness both to give and to receive is a powerful catalyst in helping people become personally involved in the expression of Christian faith.[4]

Work among young delinquents, particularly in the high-school and post-high-school ages, is no doubt the most difficult work facing the Church today. It certainly cannot be performed along older "evangelistic" lines, where young people were herded together in rallies and pressured into accepting Jesus as personal Saviour and Lord. Too many young people have already had disillusioning experiences with evangelistic phonies. Moreover, what concerns these young people is not heaven and hell, but how to get a job and keep it, how to finish high school, how to break the dope habit, and how to escape from the clutches of a gang.[5] They need a new concept of what they as individuals can be, and therefore they cannot be reached by mass communication nor rehabilitated through building recreational facilities for them. Life can be just as meaningless to them whether they loiter in a modern gym or in a shack along the railroad tracks. To reach modern delinquents one must work in depth, usually with one at a time, or at most in small groups, where they can learn to share with one another their desperations and their hopes.

METHODS OF COMMUNICATION

Certain features of communication distinguish almost all these significant movements. In the first place, just as much emphasis is given to the carrier of the information as to the content. Intuitively, this double emphasis is a recognition of what communication experts describe as the relationship between the message and the paramessage; that is to say, the verbal or symbolic content and the source and circumstances of communication. It is one thing for us to judge what is said and quite another to judge the validity of what is said on the basis of who has said it.

The content of a message is communicated by its symbols; the value of the message is communicated by the person who produces the message and the circumstances under which it is communicated. Certainly for the message of God's redeeming love of mankind, the source and circumstances are of equal importance to the content. For throughout the history of Christianity it has always been a matter of the Word and the witness, the Bible and the Church—both the content and the carrier of information are uniquely inseparable.

Since the Protestant minister and the Roman Catholic priest have been so largely isolated from the modern world[6] (they are paid to live exemplary lives in the gilded cage of their professional restrictions), it is often the layman who is in the best position to talk to laymen, just as the former alcoholic is better prepared to speak to a man who is suffering from this vicious system of socially-approved suicide. (All other forms of self-destruction are culturally frowned upon.)

These effective systems of communication lay real emphasis upon what technicians call "anticipatory feedback," which is nothing more or less than anticipating the practical and recognized needs of those who will receive the message. Talking to a juvenile delinquent about escaping hell doesn't really make sense, for usually he cannot imagine anything worse than the circumstances in which he finds himself in this life. The message of the Gospel must speak to life, not to death. If there is any real concern in the young person (that is, if he has not simply given up the race completely), it is how to get that high-school diploma, without which so many doors are automatically slammed in his face.

These modern movements of Christian concern direct their attention to what are known needs. Other problems are left for others to discuss; this intensely practical response to recognized problems is what characterizes the communication and explains so much of its effectiveness.

Moreover, the transmission of communication employed by these modern movements is highly personal and specific. It is a man-to-man kind of communication often involving group therapy, which largely rejects mass communication as being an inefficient approach to the problem. Radio and television are excellent techniques for selling soap and cereal, and they may serve to "soften up" a hostile audience, but they do not carry the impact of personal conviction about values.

Another significant feature of communication is the emphasis upon loyalty to an individual rather than acceptance of theological content. Loyalty is expressed on two levels: first, the loyalty of an individual to the person who has communicated to him the elements of his new faith; but primarily, of course, the loyalty of the individual to Jesus Christ, who has made this new life possible. For the most part there is no attempt to provide an intellectual undergirding or even a reasoned basis—certainly not in the initial stages of communication. Understanding is regarded as something which follows, not precedes, experience. In a sense this is what Jesus tried to explain in saying, "He that wills to do my will will know the doctrine" (John 7:17).

Still another characteristic is the de-emphasis on organization. In fact, the organizational structures of such movements are normally minimal, and where some organization is obviously required to provide for the association of persons, the organizational features are sketchy. There is usually no such thing as "membership," and certainly no statistical emphasis.

## THEOLOGICAL ASPECTS OF COMMUNICATION

Though there is diversity in the theological emphasis of various dynamic modern Christian movements, certain fundamental aspects of their communication are amazingly similar. In the first place, these movements take the Scriptures seriously. Not that they deal with critical problems of the Scriptures, nor that they are concerned with proving the inerrancy of Holy Writ. Nor can their approach to the Scriptures be described as primarily "devotional." Rather, the Bible is used as a practical set of guidelines for day-to-day living. Men read the Scriptures to find out what God is saying. Not that reading the Scriptures in this way means extracting some striking phrase from the context to justify some particular kind of behavior; nor does it mean a blind opening of the Bible and putting one's finger on a verse for "guidance for the day." Present-day Biblical renewal involves a more rational and effective use of the Bible; for people are increasingly concerned with the broad emphasis of the Scriptures, not with mere proof-texts or favorite phrases.

It is true that some persons interpret the Scriptures so literally and uncritically that their use of the Bible is open to serious danger. However, since most persons involved in modern movements of Biblical renewal are interested in the practical application of the Scriptures to their own lives, they are largely protected from theological excess. For example, one college fraternity man admitted frankly that he did not understand all that was involved in Peter's vision of the sheet coming down from heaven, but he concluded that what was meant was that a Christian had no right to blackball anyone.

Not only do these modern movements in Christian communication take the Bible seriously; they also take God seriously, with special emphasis upon a personal relationship with God in terms of the action of the Holy Spirit within the individual's life. Interestingly enough, no attempt is made to prove or to explain God. No one is concerned about His essence, but rather about what God does. Primarily it is the activity of a God who enters history in the work of the Holy Spirit in the lives of individuals which concerns these present-day Christian movements.

In keeping with this avoidance of trying to prove or argue a particular position, one finds also a tendency to avoid intellectual explanations. Not that such groups are anti-intellectual; they are primarily practical and pragmatic. The challenge is not to prove and to reason, but to test by experience. Because of this attitude, persons in such groups are not infrequently criticized as theologically naïve and religiously shallow. However, it is possible that this attitude is the childlike confidence and trust which Jesus himself commended.

Another important emphasis in these contemporary Christian movements is the approach to the total life of man. No longer does one speak of saving men's souls, but of saving the man. At the same time, it is not assumed that perfection is to be arrived at all at once. In fact, the approach is essentially a step-by-step orientation, with no attempt to achieve victory over all problems by one supreme act of dedication, but rather to conquer one difficulty after another in a day-by-day approach. One does not claim to be cured of alcoholism for life, but rather to have gained victory over the problem for that particular day.

Perhaps the most striking phenomenon in these contemporary Christian movements is the lack of fixed formulas. There are few rules and regulations, and usually no rigid structuring of content. Even the leaders themselves say that they are often at a loss to explain exactly what is happening. Moreover, they sense that if they do organize and structure the details of their program, they are very likely to fail, for then it will be impossible to respond creatively to new situations.

Here are typical circumstances in which new wine is looking for new bottles.

CRITICISMS OF MODERN MOVEMENTS

These modern Christian movements, which seem to be so dynamic, and yet are so amorphous and difficult to categorize, have naturally come in for a large measure of severe criticism, particularly from those in well-entrenched positions or those who see in such movements a threat to ecclesiastical traditions. In the first place, these movements are criticized as not being theologically grounded. Certainly one does not find the old creedal statements, and in the meetings of such groups the old answers just are not given. Little is said, for example, about verbal inspiration, and almost nothing about inerrancy. Moreover, such movements rarely, if ever, have doctrinal statements which members and speakers must sign.

But if such movements are denounced by the traditional right, they are equally criticized by the liberal left; for to those theologians who really believe that "God is dead," the communication of those who take seriously both the Scriptures *and* God seems to be unutterably naïve. However, for these laymen God is not dead, nor has He ever been near death, since the majority of these persons never had a false picture of God which had to die in order for a new concept to develop.

Possibly one of the problems for modern iconoclastic theologians, who think they must tear down the whole structure of theology in order to rebuild, is that they themselves have suffered from an inadequate view of God. This concept, in the philosophical maelstrom of modern life, *did* die. Emotionally and psychologically, therefore, these theologians have experienced the death of their God. However, most modern secular people have not gone through this kind of experience, and accordingly do not feel the psychological necessity of proclaiming the demise of God. They admit they do not understand God, but they are perfectly willing to act on the assumption that God does exist if He gives every proof of meeting their practical needs as no other power can or does. Perhaps, in a sense, the viewpoints represented by these modern lay movements are more Biblical than those of some theologians; for their emphasis, like that of the Bible, is upon a God who acts, rather than one who merely exists.[7] A personal encounter with this God is precisely the essence of Biblical experience, and a refusal to go beyond the Bible in defining faith may be the best guarantee of avoiding modern paganism. The absence of classical statements about their faith may mean that these persons have avoided concepts which really come from the classical philosophies of Plato and Aristotle rather than from the radical realism of the Bible. Here, essentially, is Existentialism in its Biblical, rather than in its philosophical, garb.

A second criticism of these movements is their failure to be ecclesiastically oriented; that is to say, they neither ask nor accept direction by the existing church leadership.[8] Certainly they are not the result of some thought-out plan by church commissions, nor are they the product of committee resolutions. However, in the past vital movements in Christianity have not grown at the ecclesiastical peak, but rather have normally been outgrowths and shoots from the base. In other words, Christianity does not grow like a pine tree at its hierarchical pinnacle, but like a banana plant, which sends out shoots that constantly furnish new life and vigor at the base, once the existing structure has reached maturity and has begun to die.

Though some of these modern movements appear to be antichurch, those which are doing the most creative work are not truly so. They sometimes are peripheral to the church, however, for the church often lacks the kind of structure which readily admits new and dynamic developments.

Some pastors are understandably suspicious of these developments, for too much activity on the part of laymen would seem to jeopardize the professional security of the clergy. However, such movements are not strictly of the laity, for there are many ministers involved; moreover, they are not anticlerical. They may be seen as movements that have not

yet found a way to relate their dynamic faith to the life of
the church. In some ways, however, this meeting of small
groups of dedicated persons, to share their faith and to express
it in concrete action, is as close a parallel to first-century
Christianity as has developed since the Reformation.

A third criticism, and one readily understandable, is that
these movements are too much oriented to the here and now,
with little or no attention to heaven and hell, life and death,
judgment and eternal life. On the other hand, if eternal life
is really of a different quality, and not merely an extension of
life ("he who has the Son hath life"), then this new kind of
life should begin now. Certainly the traditional picture of
heavenly bliss—sitting on a cloud stringing a harp—has little
appeal to modern activist man. Moreover, in this very emphasis upon the here and now, upon "the kingdom of God within
you," and upon the Christian life to be lived *in* the world,
while not being *of* it—such movements are intensely Biblical.[9]

### PROBLEMS IN COMMUNICATION

Despite the many essentially Biblical elements in the dynamic
communication of these contemporary Christian movements,
certain real problems inevitably arise in such movements, as
in any other communication. These are conditioned by the
very nature of communication itself; for what is involved is
not merely what a source may encode or produce, but also
what a receptor must decode and assimilate. This receiving
process is conditioned by three distinct processes: (1) selectivity, (2) skewing, and (3) restructuring.

### SELECTIVITY

Whether a receptor assimilates a message depends in very
large measure upon the selective process involved. Most persons, for example, simply do not "listen to" or "take in" a
message which is unacceptable to them. For example, a woman
incurably ill with cancer repeatedly went back to her doctor

to be told what was wrong with her. On each occasion he explained carefully that she had a form of cancer which could not be cured. However, by the next day, in speaking to friends and relatives, she complained bitterly that no one would tell her what was wrong with her, not even her doctor. So efficient had her selective process become that she simply did not remember anything that she did not want to retain. Similarly, some persons can be told in incontrovertible ways that the condemnation of Ham in the Genesis account has nothing to do with Negroes, for Negroes are not Hamites in any biological or cultural sense; but such statements simply fall on deaf ears because of the emotionally-controlled selective system.

Selectivity may also be conditioned by existing ideas which block the entrance of new concepts. If, for example, a man is convinced that miracles cannot happen, then the Biblical accounts of miracles will be selectively rejected. Such selectivity may even apply to minor details of Biblical exegesis. For example, some hyperdispensationalists are so convinced that "the law" has passed away that they cannot bring themselves to translate literally the passage: "Till heaven and earth pass away, not an iota, not a dot, will pass from the law until all is accomplished" (RSV).

Selectivity also operates in areas of incomprehension. That is to say, if we cannot understand what is being talked about, we normally reject the message. The average reader, for example, of Colossians 1:16 (RSV), in which Paul speaks of "thrones or dominions or principalities or authorities," simply bypasses the concepts involved, since he has no intellectual pigeonhole into which they fit. Lacking a conceptual structure of neo-Platonism, with its nine orders of spirit powers in three groups of three each, on which the passage is based, he rejects this particular communication.

## SKEWING

While selection may provide a basis both for rejection and for acceptance, skewing is a process by which certain concepts are filtered in, but are altered in the process of being accepted. For example, modern psychological interpretations of human behavior prompt many people to reinterpret demonic possession as simply psychoneurotic behavior. Similarly, for the warlike, primitive Guaica in the jungles of southern Venezuela, the portrayal of Jesus in the Garden of Gethsemane becomes completely skewed as the result of Guaica values; for they cannot conceive of anyone's being such a fool or such a coward as to let himself be captured or refuse to fight.

The coloring of new ideas as the result of existing concepts is, of course, typical for all peoples. The thought of having to marry one's sister-in-law may be distasteful to the average man in the Western world; but in societies where levirate marriage is practiced (it was also a pattern in Old Testament times) such a custom is taken for granted. On the other hand, while we readily accept the idea of a man and woman from different areas and family backgrounds setting up a new nuclear family, with little or no attachment to their respective families, such a practice is regarded as reprehensible in many African societies. When on one occasion a missionary explained to a Kaka chieftain in the Cameroun that he was born at least two months' journey from the home of his wife, and that they had met in a school at least three months' journey away, and that at last they had started their own family in Africa at least one year's journey from their previous homes (distance was in each instance calculated in terms of canoe travel and walking on foot—the only system which would make sense in Kaka society), the chieftain said: "Ah, I see! White men are just like fish. They lay their eggs and sperm and then go off to let their offspring float away downstream. Yes, white people are just as senseless as fish."

### RESTRUCTURING

Basic presuppositions result not only in selecting and skewing of information, but in complete restructuring, particularly as various components are put together into new combinations.[10]

This is precisely what has happened in the history of Christianity. The institution of the Communion began as a reflection of Old Testament covenant practice in eating the covenant meal; but within a relatively short time the Communion was transformed into a fertility cult practice, where Christ, as the God, was slain each time the Mass was celebrated and people ate of his body and blood. Such restructuring can readily take place in any Christian context where old and new ideas undergo mutual readjustment. Among the Patamuna of British Guiana pre-Christian practices of cursing employed "powerful words"—unknown words supposed to have overwhelming spirit power. When missionaries came among the Patamuna, they did not normally learn the language, but spoke through interpreters. The interpreters themselves, unable to translate all the Christian expressions, simply transliterated words like *temptation, wicked, devil, Christmas, conversion,* and *salvation.* However, since these words were not really understood, they were considered to be "powerful words"— those mysterious, unknown expressions associated with religion which had tremendous spirit power. At present, the form of cursing among the Patamuna has changed, for no longer are the pre-Christian "powerful words" used. Rather, the Christian ones are used, and cursing becomes relatively easy, for as one Patamuna explained, "Now a person can go to prayer meeting, kneel behind the one whom he wishes to curse, and while everyone is praying out loud, he can mutter these 'powerful words' and thus destroy his enemy."

### ANSWERS—REAL AND UNREAL

Because of the inherent dangers in communication, whether by selectivity, skewing, or restructuring, it is understandable that many have felt that two things were necessary to guard against abuse of communication: first, one must insist that the whole structure of belief be understood, and secondly, a critical attitude must be avoided.

By prefabricating a set of beliefs to prevent doctrinal impurity, it has been assumed that religious faith could be so structured as to guarantee orthodoxy. Accordingly, Christianization was thought to consist essentially in teaching the structure of this prefabricated faith. Once it was learned (usually memorized in the form of a catechism), and then formally adopted, with confirmation of this fact registered in baptism, confirmation, or church membership, the Christian was presumably safe from the wiles of Satan and the temptations of the flesh. But this simply is not true. One cannot live in a prefabricated faith. Faith has to be built by the one who has it. Moreover, faith cannot be inherited, for, as it has been aptly said, "God has many children, but no grandchildren." Unfortunately, what we often interpret as desertion of a man's faith is really not desertion at all. What a man has given up is not his own faith, but a faith prepared for him by someone else. He has not lost his own faith in God; he has merely rejected another's explanations of God.

While some will admit that "precooked" faith is not only unpalatable, but usually indigestible, they still feel that, in these uncertain days in which we live, when doubt is rampant, we cannot afford to be critical or to question sacred traditions. As one missionary insisted: "I wish Christians were as loyal to Christianity as Buddhists are to Buddhism. When we raise questions about Christianity, we only injure people's faith." It is true, of course, that Buddhism, Hinduism, and Islam have never experienced the intense degree of self-criticism characteristic of Christianity, particularly since the Reformation. In fact, some have insisted that Islam would fall apart if the same techniques of literary criticism were applied to the Koran as have been applied to the Bible. But this is not only wishful thinking but erroneous analysis. The great liability of non-Christian faiths is not the possibility of self-criticism, but the lack of such criticism, with the result that the traditional institutions of these religions have become completely unresponsive to the demands of modern life. On the other hand, a renewal of Christian faith always involves a measure of criticism, for new wine always breaks old bottles, and we are inevitably forced to ask why the old bottles have broken. Biblical faith inevitably destroys theological idols—those formulations which go beyond Scripture and which presume to explain the inexplicable, to eliminate paradoxes, and to prove why God acted as He did. This has always been a favorite preoccupation of man for reducing God to man's image, and has always been the best way of seeming to control God. Having carved Him out to the contours of our verbal definitions, we think we can make God more predictable, or at least more philosophically controllable. Thus with idols of words we imitate the pagan who makes images of wood.

Modern iconoclasm—the breaking of idols—has taken two principal forms: iconoclasm against traditional extra-Biblical verbal formulas; and iconoclasm against ecclesiastical institutions which seem incapable of adjusting themselves to modern needs. But while the iconoclast may serve a certain useful function, a far more important role is performed by one who shows the way to Biblical renewal and relevance, and who provides new wine which will automatically break old bottles and because of its value demand and receive new ones.

# 6

# FROM GOD
# TO MAN

In view of the dynamic relevance in the communication of Christian faith, one may well ask why the Church has not experienced greater response to its message. If the Biblical account of God and man can successfully capture the thinking of so many people, why has Christian faith nevertheless been restricted to a minority? Moreover, in our present world the claims of this faith are regarded as in no sense unique as compared with the claims of other religious systems. Thus comparability gives rise to belief in ultimate relativism and universalism. A century or more ago the Christian could feel somewhat secure in his traditional and often untested beliefs, for he was insulated by space, time, and cultural-linguistic barriers from the rest of the world. But now religious isolationism is as impossible as political isolationism. As members of the human family we are "in one world"—to make it livable or to perish together.

## COMMUNICATION — CHRISTIAN AND NON-CHRISTIAN

In order to understand certain essential features of religious communication, it is important to contrast several basic elements of Christian and non-Christian communication. This can best be done by noting their divergent features in parallel columns.

| CHRISTIAN FAITH | NON-CHRISTIAN FAITH |
|---|---|
| 1. God takes the initiative in opening up the dialogue. | 1. Man takes the initiative in seeking God. |
| 2. The barrier to communication is man's sin (or alienation). | 2. The barrier to communication is God's preoccupation. |
| 3. The prerequisite to communication is man's repentance and reconciliation. | 3. The prerequisite to communication is specialized knowledge. |
| 4. God responds to man, for he is already predisposed to do so. | 4. God responds to man largely out of duress, because he is compelled or propitiated. |
| 5. God gives all for nothing— divine grace. | 5. The transaction between man and God is essentially contractual—a *quid pro quo* arrangement. |
| 6. Man seeks to know and do God's will. | 6. Man seeks to have God do man's will. |

Certain phases of these contrasted aspects of communication require further explanation.

1. *Initiative.* From the Biblical viewpoint, God always begins the conversation. It was He who conversed with man in the Garden of Eden, who addressed His messages to men through the prophets, and who took the initiative in sending His Son Jesus Christ into the world. By way of contrast, non-Biblical faiths emphasize man's seeking out

God or ultimate reality; and though man may receive special revelation, it is normally in response to man's initial preparation. Apart from the Biblical faiths, only in Islam does one encounter the Biblical view of God as having taken the initiative.

2. *Barriers to communication.*   In the Biblical view, man's sin results in his being alienated from God. That is to say, man's basic rebellion compels him to withdraw from God, and thus it is man's sin which constitutes a primary barrier to communication. In contrast, most non-Biblical faiths represent God as being essentially preoccupied, either with His personal affairs or with running the world. In the Old Testament account of Elijah and the prophets of Baal, this basic contrast is well exemplified, for Elijah taunts the false prophets by insisting that they cry louder and gash themselves more deeply in order to attract the attention of their gods. In most religions, God's attention can ultimately be obtained, but it is usually a difficult, wearisome, and sometimes very expensive process.

3. *Prerequisite to communication.* If, in Biblical Christianity, man's sins are the barrier to communication, it is man's repentance which becomes a prerequisite to communication. On the other hand, in most non-Christian faiths, the prerequisite to communication with the divine is specialized knowledge. That is to say, one must know precisely how to address the deity, what prayers and incantations are most propitious for particular occasions, and what gifts and sacrifices emphasize best the urgency of one's request.

4. *God's predisposition.*   Biblical Christianity insists that God is predisposed to answer man's requests. That is to say, God knows even before we ask, and as a loving Father He is already disposed to provide what is good for His children. On the other hand, non-Christian faiths usually depict the deity as reluctant to grant benefits. The gods seem quite ready to punish men for lack of ritual observance, but to provide benefits they must usually be compelled by proper

rites and generous gifts. In other words, the gods normally act out of duress. Moreover, the greater the benefit sought, the greater must be the gift to the deity, so that in extreme examples, to save life in the face of some major plague, even human life itself must be sacrificed in order for the gods to act on behalf of man.

5. *God's response.* In the New Testament view, God's response is essentially all for nothing; that is to say, the unmerited favor of what is theologically called "grace." In non-Christian faiths, however, the essential relationship is a contract, neatly summarized in the Latin formula *Do ut des,* literally, "I give in order that you may give." In general, however, man usually tries to strike the better bargain. For example, he pours out a cup of liquor for his patron deity, while he himself drinks the rest of the bottle; or he sprinkles the blood of freshly killed game on the hunting shrine, while he prepares for a feast.

6. *God's will.* The Biblical view of the ultimate purpose in religious life is that man might seek to know and do God's will. In most circumstances other faiths present quite a different picture of religious purpose; that is, religion is primarily a technique whereby man seeks to constrain God, that is, to have God do man's will.

A careful view of the image of god as presented by non-Christian faiths shows a god constructed essentially in the image of man; basically, a half-man-and-half-god potentate, superior to man in power, but essentially human in the irresponsible ways in which such power is displayed or brought to bear upon human problems.

### PAGANIZED CHRISTIANITY

If Christian faith does possess the essentially unique features which have been suggested as distinctive of Biblical Christianity, one may well ask why these unique characteristics are not more fully recognized. The real reason, no doubt, is the fact that Christianity is usually presented, not in its essential Biblical form, but rather in its paganized counterpart. Certainly the average preacher, rather than announcing the presence and power of God, either in his words or in his life, gives an impression of trying to find God somewhere. One unique feature of Jesus' ministry was the evident way in which people associated his life and ministry with the presence of God among men.

From the way in which many Christians pray, one would certainly assume that the major difficulty in obtaining an answer to prayer is God's "pre-occupation." In the first place, prayer often becomes a kind of not-so-subtle teasing of the divine, for the typical "gimme" prayers crowd out genuine worship. Even specialized knowledge receives a high priority in Christendom, where increasingly it is only the minister or the priest who is thought to be able to pray correctly. In churches where "Thou" and "Thee" are thought to be the only appropriate forms for addressing the Deity, many laymen are reluctant to pray, since they feel they cannot use these linguistically proper forms in such a way that either God will be pleased or others will approve. Even the specialized intonations used in praying would suggest that God is psychologically very distant and only unusual verbal means can attract His attention.

Theoretically, Christians do not claim that God acts under duress or compulsion, but actually they behave as if they thought God could be compelled either by man's personal piety or by his ritual observance. For example, some persons feel that if they attend church regularly and tithe consistently God is automatically placed under obligation to them and therefore must prosper them in business. When things go wrong, they immediately complain, "I've always been good. Why does God do this to me?" When, however, personal piety fails to produce significant economic rewards for the church, then bazaars, food sales, and even bingo are brought in to supply the lack.

Some Christians insist that they are thoroughly Biblical in their prayers, since they always use the phrase "in the name of Jesus," despite the fact that the content of their prayers may be thoroughly self-centered or organization-centered. Far more complex, however, is the difficulty posed by the highly structured plans of Christian organizations, which rarely take into consideration any significant or dynamic movement of the Spirit of God. As one man has aptly put it, "The Holy Spirit would have to wait for at least five years in our denomination, for we are simply too well organized to permit any interruption in our present five-year plan."

The complaints which men so frequently level against Christianity are essentially not criticisms of Biblical Christianity, but of a paganized form of Christian faith.[1]

### WHAT IS CHRISTIAN FAITH?

Christian faith has been traditionally defined in terms of a set of propositions, generally in a creed or a catechism, but sometimes in the more elaborate form of a systematic theology. Such verbal definitions of Christianity are, however, only descriptions of reality, not the real thing; for reality is the experience of man's relationship to God, not the description of how, why, and where such an experience takes place.[2] In brief, theology is to religion what grammar is to a language. In the same way that one may know the grammar of a language without knowing the language—that is to say, without being able to communicate by means of it—so one may know the theology of a religion without having personal experience within the religious context.

Biblical Christianity, however, is far more than any mere acceptance of creedal propositions. It is essentially loyalty to a person, namely, Jesus Christ, without whom there is simply no such thing as Christianity. But loyalty to a person is more than mere interpersonal adherence. It involves a radical change in one's total value system, for the follower of Christ is *in* the world, but he is not *of* it. That is to say, his values are not typical of the world system, and as a "spiritual man," that is, one sensitive to the Spirit of God, he is not dominated by the values of the "natural man."

## THE ANALOGY OF COMPUTERS

Computers, often regarded as "simulated brains," provide us with some significant analogies in the area of human behavior and values. Of course, the computer is in no sense the equivalent of the human brain, which is at least one hundred thousand times more complex than any computer that has ever been designed, assuming, that is, that each brain cell is able to store one so-called "bit" (binary unit of information). However, neurophysiologists now claim that each nerve cell is a kind of miniature computer in and of itself, and that it may store almost incredible quantities of information. But whatever the degree of physical and chemical complexity of the human brain, it is certainly true that if one were to construct with transistors a computer with anything like the complexity of the human brain, it could not be stored in a building the size of the Empire State Building in New York. This means that something incredibly complex and extensive is encased within the human skull.

Nevertheless, computers are able to make some very remarkable computations with incredible speed, though restricted essentially to answering questions involving A and B, A or B, both A and B, neither A nor B, A is to B as C is to D. What the computer cannot say is "Phooey!" In other words, the computer has no built-in value system. To this extent it is radically different from the human brain, which in all circumstances places a value tag upon every experience registered in the human brain.

## A VALUE GRID

The fact that the human brain always places a value tag upon experience is the one thing that makes man unique, and certainly radically different from a computer. The physiological structure of the brain may of course be compared with the mechanical components of a computer, and the functioning of the brain is similar to the computer programming. But there is nothing in the computer analogous to the value grid through which all experience may be said to pass before it is recorded in the memory. The fact that such values do exist in a relatively complex hierarchy is well illustrated when people are forced to "act before they think," for under such circumstances their essential values are immediately revealed.

A typical value grid might be represented as in Figure 13.

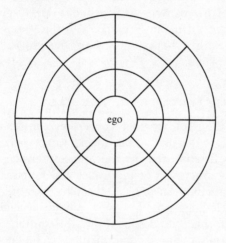

Figure 13

This type of value grid has as its center the human ego, and values are assigned in proportion as the ego is satisfied. Of course, the ego becomes conditioned by the cultural experience of the individual and his relationship to the broader social context in which he lives, but the values he registers are his own.[3]

In a sense, Christianity can be described functionally in terms of a complete substitution of the center of one's value system. That is to say, substituting for ego (even in its culturally modified form) at the center of human personality, Christ becomes this new center, with a resulting radical alteration in values.[4] This is what the Bible talks about when it speaks of "old things passing away and all things becoming new." This was essentially the experience of Paul, who saw that what he had cherished before became worthless to him, and what before seemed like rubbish became highly prized. In the process of conversion the individual does not, of course, forget his past experience, but it becomes radically reinterpreted as the result of having an entirely new value center.

Conversion does not result in immediate and complete alteration of the patterns of life, but it does begin a lifelong process, described in the Bible as "sanctification," which provides man with a basis for learning the implications of his new value system.

### RESTRUCTURING THE VALUE GRID

It is one thing to say that conversion consists in radically altering the center of the individual's value system, and quite another to describe the dynamic process involved in such a wholesale restructuring of life values and purposes. To obtain such a restructuring many societies have used numerous techniques, including social pressure, physical coercion, popular appeal, charismatic leadership, "thought control," and authoritarian education. But though all these techniques may result in significant degrees of outward conformity, they do not result in men's being actually transformed. Love is the only power sufficient to achieve a radical change in human personality. It is significant that only in Christianity is love chosen as the unique means by which man is to be transformed, for "we love God since he first loved us." And it is "the love of Christ which constrains men."

Perhaps a personal illustration from the writer's own life may illustrate this matter. Like most college men he was interested in dating, but even after a lovely evening with an attractive companion, he generally reacted to the expenditure involved by thinking that he could have bought a couple of books for the same amount of money. When he was "going steady," he tried his best to make as big an impression as possible with the least expenditure of money. This, of course, did not result in his being any great social success, but it was clear indication of his essential value system.

Some years later, however, when he fell genuinely in love, all of this was changed immediately; for instead of trying to determine how big an impression he could make on a limited amount of money, his whole concern was trying to determine just what would make his fiancée happiest, irrespective of the amount of money involved.

Divine love operates in a somewhat analogous, but much more profound manner. On one occasion, for example, a young man dashed into the Bible Society office in Minneapolis, demanding a list of Protestant beliefs, for he said that he had a Protestant girl friend and he wanted to prove that she was entirely wrong. The clerk in the store urged the young man to buy a New Testament as the best way to determine what Protestants believe. The young man made the purchase and quickly left. Some months later he returned—a very different young man. Among other things, he said, "I never dreamed that a man could love like that man Jesus." This love of God as expressed in Jesus Christ has always been the unique appeal of Biblical Christianity.

### GOD LOVES

In general, people tend to reject the concept of God's love as being a vital force in the world, for love seems weak and ineffective in contrast with the brutal realities of physical force. In fact, if people do believe that God loves, they often conclude that He does so primarily because He can do nothing else. Certainly God as one who loves is not the picture which most people have of Him, as is so obvious when they describe what they would do if they were only God. Under such circumstances people insist that they would punish certain persons, destroy others, do away with certain institutions, and force widespread reforms. In other words, they would act in a completely authoritarian and totalitarian manner, for to be God is seemingly to be a dictator. Instinctively people seem to think that dictators are strong, and therefore they can act in irresponsible ways. In reality, of course, dictators are totalitarian not because they are really strong, but because they are essentially weak.[5] Since they possess the willing support of only a minority of those whom they seek to control, they must force conformity.

God chooses to love man not out of weakness but as the result of his sovereign strength. God's love, however, is not in any way equivalent to human sentimentality or emotional attachment, for the love of God is the love which suffers. God suffers primarily because He does love, for genuine love always demands complete freedom in the object of its love. It is this insistence upon freedom which causes genuine suffering. If a man really loves a woman, he will always provide her with the opportunity of saying a genuine "no" as well as a "yes," for it is the essence of love not to compel acceptance but to respect the freedom of the object of one's love. Therefore, God refuses to manipulate man like a puppet in a show or a marionette on strings. Furthermore, God will not even stack the cards in His own favor so as to rule out man's genuine acceptance or ultimate rejection. This is no idle game with God, whereby He provides man with seeming freedom on earth, only to engulf Him later in the enforced acceptance preached by universalism. God insists upon man's freedom, even with eternal consequences.

The story of the Prodigal Son is often interpreted merely in terms of what happens to a young man who squanders his inheritance in riotous living. Others see in this story a judgment upon the self-righteousness of the elder brother. But this parable also reveals an essential truth about the father. In fact, the easiest thing for the father to have done was to have sent his servants, or even to have gone himself, into the far country to find his son, bail him out, and bring him home. However, the father loved his son too much to do so. In fact, he loved him so much that he was willing to wait until his son had come to the end of himself. This is the love which risks the suffering of rejection.

## A NEW CONCEPT OF THE CHRISTIAN COMMUNICATOR

Christianity as a way of life can only be communicated meaningfully in a living context by persons who have not only discovered the uniqueness of their faith but have been captured by the love that led to the cross. Too often in the past this love of God has been associated with the idea of "gentle Jesus, meek and mild," with the conclusion that Christians should be more or less harmless nonentities, enjoying their personal piety in relative seclusion from the harsh world of reality. This, however, is certainly not Biblical Christianity, for early Christians were willing to love God to the point of suffering the consequences of their new-found faith. Moreover, they loved others to the point of depriving themselves. These were the people who were "turning the world upside down"—a far cry from the play-it-safe security sought by many Christians today. Rather, however, than be the spiritual counterpart of Mr. Milquetoast, the true communicator of Christian faith is characterized by three fundamental attributes. In the first place, he is incredibly courageous. Knowing that the ultimate victory is God's, he feels dispensable. In the fight for alleviating human suffering, righting social wrongs, and ministering to man's deepest spiritual needs, no force nor pressure can stop him.

In the second place, the real Christian is absurdly happy. That is to say, his happiness seems to have absolutely no human justification. This is not the happiness of exuberant hilarity, but of divine enthusiasm—the heritage of a man who has found meaning in life.

The third conspicuous characteristic of the real Christian

is the fact that he is always in trouble for righteousness' sake. Any man determined to right wrong in the tradition of the Old Testament prophets or of the Son of Man can never be wholly popular. Unfortunately, one would get the impression from some books of advice to Christian ministers that it was Dale Carnegie who wrote the New Testament as a book about how to win friends and influence people.[6] But it was Jesus who said, "Woe to you when all men speak well of you, for so did their fathers of the false prophets." Furthermore, "Blessed are you when you are persecuted for righteousness' sake." This is the kind of religious faith which refuses to make the church a mere religious adjunct to the Country Club. The man with the truly prophetic message is "out of step with the world,"[7] but he cannot be silenced, for any man who has experienced the love of God and the resulting freedom which comes from reconciliation cannot turn his back on the promptings of God's Spirit. He cannot keep this divine constraint to himself any more than the early church could, whose members defied civil and religious authorities and rejoiced that they "were counted worthy of suffering for his name." It was this contagious new quality of life which men discovered as the result of having been with Jesus, for in him they found what it meant to deny oneself, to take up one's cross and go to one's own Calvary in the steps of the Master. At last, having discovered someone worth dying for, they found something worth living for. The communication of love had given meaning to life.

# Bibliography

Berelson, Bernard and Gary A. Steiner. 1964. *Human Behavior: An Inventory of Scientific Findings*. New York: Harcourt, Brace and World, Inc.

Berger, Peter L. 1961. *The Noise of Solemn Assemblies*. Garden City, N. Y.: Doubleday and Co.

Berton, Pierre. 1965. *The Comfortable Pew*. Philadelphia and New York: J. B. Lippincott Co.

Bonhoeffer, Dietrich. 1954. *Prisoner for God*. New York: Macmillan Co.

———. 1959. *Ethics* (Tr. by Neville H. Smith). London: S.C.M. Press.

Buber, Martin. 1937. *I and Thou* (Tr. by Ronald G. Smith). Edinburgh: T. and T. Clark.

Bultmann, Rudolf. 1951, 1955. *Theology of the New Testament* (2 vols.) (Tr. by Kendrick Grobel). New York: Charles Scribner's Sons.

Campbell, Joseph. 1959. *The Masks of God: Primitive Mythology*. New York: Viking Press.

———. 1962. *The Masks of God: Oriental Mythology*. London: Secker and Warburg.

———. 1964. *The Masks of God: Occidental Mythology*. New York: Viking Press.

Cox, Harvey. 1965. *The Secular City*. New York: The Macmillan Co.

Cragg, Kenneth. 1965. *The Call of the Minaret*. New York: Oxford University Press.

Edwards, David L. and John A. T. Robinson, eds. 1963. *The Honest to God Debate*. London: S.C.M. Press.

Eliade, Mircea. 1954. *Cosmos and History*. New York: Harper & Row.

Frankl, Viktor. 1963. *Man's Search for Meaning*. Boston: Beacon Press.

Glock, Charles Y., and Rodney Stark. 1965. "Is There an American Protestantism?" *Trans-Action*. Nov.-Dec. pp. 8–13, 48–49.

Hatt, Paul K., and Albert J. Reill, Jr., eds. 1951. *Cities and Society*. Glencoe, Ill.: The Free Press.

Herberg, Will. 1955. *Protestant-Catholic-Jew*. Garden City, N. Y.: Doubleday and Co.

Jensen, Adolf E. 1963. *Myth and Cult Among Primitive Peoples* (Tr. by M. T. Choldin and W. Weissleder). Chicago and London: University of Chicago Press.

Kerr, Walter. 1962. *The Decline of Pleasure*. New York: Simon and Schuster.

Kluckhohn, Clyde, and Henry A. Murray, eds. 1949. *Personality in Nature, Society, and Culture*.

Lee, Robert, ed. 1962. *Cities and Churches*. Philadelphia: The Westminster Press.

Loescher, Frank S. 1948. *The Protestant Church and the Negro, A Pattern of Segregation*. New York: Association Press.

Loukes, Harold. 1961. *Teenage Religion*. London: S.C.M. Press.

Lynch, Kevin. 1960. *The Image of the City*. Cambridge, Mass.: The M.I.T. Press and Harvard University Press.

Lynd, Robert S. and Helen M. 1937. *Middletown in Transition*. New York: Harcourt, Brace and Co.

Malinowski, Bronislaw. 1954. *Magic, Science and Religion and Other Essays*. Garden City, N. Y.: Doubleday and Co.

Mumford, Lewis. 1940. *Faith for Living*. New York: Harcourt, Brace and Co.

———. 1961. *The City in History*. New York: Harcourt, Brace and World.

Munby, D. L. 1963. *The Idea of a Secular Society*. London: Oxford University Press

Myrdal, Gunnar, with Richard Sterner and Arnold Rose. 1944. *An American Dilemma* (2 vols.). New York: Harper & Brothers.

Nida, Eugene A., and William A. Smalley. 1959. *Introducing Animism*. New York: Friendship Press.

Nida, Eugene A. 1954. *Customs and Cultures*. New York: Harper & Row.

———. 1960. *Message and Mission*. New York: Harper & Row.

Niebuhr, H. Richard. 1963. *The Responsible Self*. New York: Harper & Row.

Packard, Vance. 1959. *The Status Seekers*. New York: David McKay Co., Inc.

Pitt, Malcolm. 1955. *Introducing Hinduism*. New York: Friendship Press.

Radin, Paul, ed. 1957. *Primitive Religion*. New York: Dover Publications, Inc.

Redfield, Robert. 1953. *The Primitive World and Its Transformations*. Ithaca, N. Y.: Cornell University Press.

Robinson, John A. T. 1963. *Honest to God*. Philadelphia: The Westminster Press.

Stacey, Nicolas. 1965. "The Decline of the Church in England." *Harper's*, March, pp. 64–70.

Tannenbaum, Frank. 1933. *Peace by Revolution*. New York: Columbia University Press.

Tawney, R. H. 1926. *Religion and the Rise of Capitalism*. New York: Harcourt, Brace and Co.

Wakefield, Dan. 1960. "Slick-Paper Christianity," in *Identity and Anxiety*, ed. by Maurice R. Stein, Arthur J. Vidich, and David Manning White. Glencoe, Ill.: The Free Press. Pp. 410–415.

Warner, Sam B., Jr. 1962. *Streetcar Suburbs*. Cambridge, Mass.: Harvard University Press and the M.I.T. Press.

Weber, Max. 1922. *The Sociology of Religion*. Boston: Beacon Press.

———. 1958. *The City*. New York: Collier Books. London: Heinemann.

———. 1958. *The Protestant Ethic and the Spirit of Capitalism*. New York: Charles Scribner's Sons. London: Allen and Unwin (Original German ed. 1904–1905).

Willetts, William. 1958. *Chinese Art* (Vol. I). New York: George Braziller, Inc.

Wilson, J. Christy. 1950. *Understanding Islam*. New York: Friendship Press.

Wright, Arthur F. 1959. *Buddhism in Chinese History*. Stanford, Calif.: Stanford U. Press.

Wright, G. Ernest, and Reginald H. Fuller. 1957. *The Book of the Acts of God*. Garden City, N. Y.: Doubleday and Company, Inc.

Yinger, J. Milton. 1957. *Religion, Society, and the Individual*. New York: Macmillan Co.

# Notes

1. Summary analyses of motivations, or drives, are to be found in Berelson and Steiner, *Human Behavior*, pp. 239–258, esp. p. 257. Rather, however, than discuss the numerous motivations listed by various psychologists, we have here chosen to group a number of these together under larger "cover terms" and then to employ a componential analysis as a means of explaining various differences of manifestation. We have not included here such an essentially biological drive as evacuation of wastes, for this is a drive which comes only as a consequence of other drives. Furthermore, we have not included the drive for "avoidance of pain," for this is primarily negative; and though it is a strong determinant of action, it can best be handled as the converse of positive drives. It is quite true that religions differ considerably in their attitudes toward pain and suffering, but motivations of avoidance are not the mainsprings of human behavior. Hence these negative drives have not been incorporated into this analysis.

Territoriality has also been described as a basic motivation, but it seems preferable to treat this as a supplementary "situational drive," i.e., a motivation to produce the kind of physical and psychological distance from other beings so as to make possible the adequate expression of the more fundamental drives which we are treating here.

2. Viktor E. Frankl, *Man's Search for Meaning*, p. 177.

3. Work and play differ primarily in terms of duress and goals. If an activity is compelled, i.e., ordered by someone else, and if the goal is something quite different from the activity, e.g., the paycheck at the end of the week, one can rightly speak of work. Note even the use of the term "workout" in speaking of the activity of a professional basketball team. One of the anomalies of American life is the incapacity of people to "play." Businessmen so often take up some sport under a sense of pressure, and engage in it, not for the sheer fun of it, but in order to gain status by improving their skill or to increase their health so they

can work harder. On the other hand, some people make a game of their work, for they engage in the activity for its own sake and not to win advancement or to take home earnings. As a result of having turned so many participation games into work (i.e., by taking the fun out of playing), we tend to turn increasingly to spectator "fun," which is neither so recreational nor so re-creative. Not knowing how to make fun out of our work, we have ended up making work out of our fun. This is in fact one of the major theses of Walter Kerr in *The Decline of Pleasure*.

4. In a set of biological-psychological drives, or motivations, one is not justified in trying to set up "pure types" at the extremes, with graded percentages between. Rather, even extremes involve mixtures, for esthetic responses possess considerable physical involvement, and the satisfying of thirst and hunger has numerous psychological overtones.

5. Cf. Harvey Cox, *The Secular City*, ch. 9: "Sex and Secularization," esp. pp. 203, 211.

6. Viktor E. Frankl, *op. cit.* Mircea Eliade, in his insightful *Cosmos and History*, suggests that precisely· this kind of meaning is provided in premodern cultures by a total participation in transcendental, primordial reality and by re-enactment of primordial events through ritual (4–5). But when the static notion of recurrent, cyclical events is replaced by a true sense of history, only *faith* in God in the Judeo-Christian sense can give man meaning that frees him from the "terror of history" (160–162).

7. Cf. Arthur F. Wright, *Buddhism in Chinese History*.

8. Cf. Malcolm Pitt, *Introducing Hinduism*.

9. Cf. R. H. Tawney, *Religion and the Rise of Capitalism*.

10. There is, of course, a sense in which ritual participation is a means for "experiencing truth," for there are important and valid uses for rites and ceremonies. However, such ritual observances cannot be any more than symbolic representations, for they are not ends in themselves but only pointers to some "referents." Their danger lies in the tendency for people to assume that the ritual symbols are goals in themselves, even as they wrongly conclude that doctrinal formulations are "truth" rather than mere descriptions of truth.

11. The emphasis upon ceremonialism, legalism, and charity (discussed in the previous section) as aggression-motivated rationaliazations of religious behavior is to be found in varying degrees and combinations in these institutionally favored solutions.

12. See Arthur F. Wright, *op. cit.*, and William Willetts, *Chinese Art*, pp. 339–348. A number of new Buddhist-based religions have developed in Japan, especially since World War II. Many of these have been extensively studied and carefully described in a quarterly journal entitled *Contemporary Religions in Japan*, published by the International Institute for the Study of Religions.

13. See Frank Tannenbaum, *Peace by Revolution*.

14. Cf. Peter L. Berger, *The Noise of Solemn Assemblies*, pp. 36–47. Cf. also this ironic observation by W. Lloyd Warner: "Although the sacred beliefs of all the seven churches of Jonesville are at war with the secular worlds of social, economic, and political power, with status inequality, and the deterioration of the mores of the community, this hostility is not always apparent in the churches' social actions" (*Democracy in Jonesville*, pp. 152 f). See also Gunnar Myrdal's statement that it was often preachers who led in reviving the Ku Klux Klan after World War I (*An American Dilemma*, p. 563).

15. Harvey Cox, *op. cit.*, pp. 207, 210.

16. Cf. R. H. Tawney, *op. cit.*

17. See Pierre Berton, *The Comfortable Pew*, pp. 90–96. Cf. also Harvey Cox: "He [Bultmann] fails to reach the man of today because he translates the Bible from mythical language into yesterday's metaphysics rather than into today's post-metaphysical lexicon" (*op. cit.*, p. 252).

18. Cf. Will Herberg's reference to the "American religion" as "an idealized description of the middle-class ethos" (*Protestant-Catholic-Jew*, p. 94); Pierre Berton: "The establishment's religion is one that calls upon the deity as a servant in peace and war . . . a 'cult of reassurance,' in which Christianity becomes a mere vehicle on the road to worldly success, and 'faith' a kind of super-aspirin that can be painlessly swallowed to provide fast, fast, fast relief from the burning issues of our times" (*op. cit.*, p. 83); also Peter L. Berger, *op. cit.*, pp. 40–45; and Robert Lee, *Cities and Churches*, p. 233, etc.

19. Arthur F. Wright, *op. cit.* p. 101.

20. Bultmann describes the syncretism between the Christian message and Hellenistic philosophy in the early centuries of the Church, but concludes: "On the whole, one could be tempted to term Hellenistic Christianity a syncretistic structure. The only reason one may not do so is that it is not just a conglomerate of

heterogeneous materials; in spite of all its syncretism in detail, it retains from its origin an inherent drive toward an independent understanding, all its own, of God, world, and man" (*Theology of the New Testament*, Vol. I, p. 164).

21. See Gunnar Myrdal, *op. cit.*, pp. 11, 458, 563; Pierre Berton, *op. cit.*, pp. 63 ff; Robert S. and Helen M. Lynd, *Middletown in Transition*, pp. 305–308.

22. Cf. Pierre Berton's statement that the modern Church tries to be both "Buddhist" and "Shintoist"; but "A Buddhist believes in the evilness and foulness of the present world and the beauty and promise of an afterlife; the Shintoist believes that the only desirable world is the present one—everything that follows is evil and foul" (*op. cit.*, pp. 56 f.).

## 2 . FROM GODS TO GHOSTS

1. In Figure 2 we have listed such spirit beings as God, gods, devil, angels, spirits, demons, gremlins and ghosts, realizing, of course, that in some societies there are far more types of such personal supernatural beings and in other religions fewer. Moreover, religions differ as to the precise order of such personal supernatural beings. This listing, however, provides at least a convenient schematic arrangement which is widely applicable.

2. There is a sense in which for many primitive peoples the supernatural world is not neatly divided between the personal and the impersonal powers (this is one reason for the wavy line between these two realms in Figure 2). For such peoples the entire universe is a type of *Thou* not *It* (cf. Robert Redfield in *The Primitive World and Its Transformations*, p. 105). On the other hand, even primitive persons make a clearer distinction between the spirits, who must decide whether or not to respond favorably to the petitioner, and the world of magic, which has no such cognitive or volitional characteristics. The powers of magic, generally regarded as blind automatic servants of the practitioner who knows the secret formulas, can thus insure results, even though the gods and spirits might be opposed.

3. This dichotomy is not the same as that popularly made between sacred and secular or profane. As Mircea Eliade says, "we might say that the archaic world knows nothing of 'profane' activities." Every meaningful act "in some way participates in the sacred" (*Cosmos and History*, pp. 27 f.).

4. This scheme may well be an effort to resolve the tension which Robert Redfield has described between the notions of predictable law and unpredictable capriciousness in nature (*op. cit.*, p. 100).

5. See Malcolm Pitt, *Introducing Hinduism*, pp. 40 ff.

6. Cf. Robert Redfield: "Nature has its sacred and personal attributes; almost any aspect of nature was thought to have its indwelling, awe-compelling force" (*op. cit.*, p. 61). For a brief but lucid description of animism, see Eugene A. Nida and William A. Smalley, *Introducing Animism*. Eliade would emphasize the notion that the events become meaningful for the premodern mind only when they cease to be unique, but are interpreted as recurrences of primordial, cosmic events. This leads to a static or rather cyclic view of the cosmos (*op. cit.*, pp. 5–7, 35–38, 96–98).

### 3 . FROM HINDUISM TO CHRISTIANITY

1. See Malcolm Pitt, *Introducing Hinduism*.

2. See Arthur F. Wright, *Buddhism in Chinese History*.

3. See William Willetts, *Chinese Art*, pp. 341–347, where the degeneration of Buddhism from a metaphysical and ascetic doctrine to a popular syncretistic polytheism—a kind of *do ut des* religion—is vividly described.

4. For a brief account of Islam, see J. Christy Wilson, *Introducing Islam*. Kenneth Cragg, in *The Call of the Minaret* and in his other writings, has described Islam more fully, but tends to give a theoretical and idealized account rather than a realistic description of popular religion.

5. Cf. Eugene A. Nida, "Mariology in Latin America," *Practical Anthropology* 4.69–82 (1957).

6. Cf. the statement of a young college graduate quoted by the Lynds: "Look, we have religion, education, and the arts in our midst. Someday we will all have time for them" (*Middletown in Transition*, p. 317). Nicholas Stacey has described "The Decline of the Church in England" (*Harper's*, March 1966, pp. 64–70). Here the people find the Church increasingly useless and superfluous in meeting their felt needs and innocuous as a challenge to Christian living. He concludes (p. 70): ". . . from all I hear and read of the American religious scene the crisis we are going through now could well be America's in a generation."

7. It is most important to distinguish clearly between "scientific

fact" and "scientism," for the former consists of the well-established findings of scientific inquiry while the latter consists of "absolutistic inferences" from such data—a procedure which genuine scientists strongly oppose. Unfortunately, the Church has too often opposed the valid results of scientific inquiry, and even today tends to maintain an obscurantist position on many vital issues.

8. Cf. Berton, *The Comfortable Pew*, p. 71.

9. Cf. Mumford's indictment of Christian anti-intellectualism: "The various articles of faith might contradict science and common sense, but people believed them triumphantly because they were incredible" (*Faith for Living*, p. 135).

10. Cf. the confusion in people's minds which is revealed in Charles Y. Glock and Rodney Stark's article "Is There an American Protestantism?" (*Trans-Action*, November-December 1965), and even more in Harold Loukes, *Teenage Religion*. The latter relates to England, but the situation is at least as bad in America.

### 4 · FROM MEDIEVAL TO MODERN MAN

1. It is recognized that any such schematically structured explanation of historical developments inevitably involves a degree of distortion, for the actual events contain multidimensional elements. However, it is still possible and legitimate to highlight certain processes in history by this method, if, of course, one bears constantly in mind the "partial picture" which is involved.

2. R. H. Tawney says, for example, "Intellectually religious opinion endorsed to the full the static view. . . . Naturally therefore, they denounced agitation. . . . Practically, the Church was an immense vested interest" (*Religion and the Rise of Capitalism*, p. 56). See also the excellent account of the dominance of the Church in medieval cities in Lewis Mumford, *The City in History*, pp. 265–269 and 316–317.

3. Cf. R. H. Tawney, *op. cit.*, pp. 67–70. It is significant that, as Tawney notes, the Reformers, and especially Luther, viewed the radical changes of their period negatively and resisted strongly (pp. 81 ff). But "Calvin, with all his rigor, accepted the main institutions of a commercial civilization" (p. 94).

4. Cf. Mumford's description of the climate of the Age of Enlightenment: "Though the institutional forms of religion dried

up, and for a large part of the population became, in the eighteenth century, a mere husk of habit, the inner aroma of Jewish morals and Christian belief pervaded the air of the Enlightenment" (*Faith for Living*, p. 18).

5. It is essential that one distinguish carefully between biological and social evolutionary theories. While general consensus, even by many Christian scholars, applies to the former, there are radical differences of opinion with respect to the latter. That is to say, so-called deterministic explanations have been much more widely applied to biological developments than to historical ones.

6. Cf. Mumford's remark that "The Theologian's Heaven took new form as the secular thinker's Future" (*Faith for Living*, p. 19).

7. This may well mean, of course, that modern man is not exposed to any relevant religious communication to which he might respond meaningfully—either because the communicators do not perceive reality (cf. Berger's remark: "Relevance presupposes a perception of the real situation. . . . in the absence of perception, however, it is only possible to uphold an ideology which is irrelevant to the facts of the matter" [*The Noise of Solemn Assemblies*, p. 37]); or because as Berton claims (*op. cit.*, pp. 92, 103) those who try to communicate do not understand the methods and means of communication.

## 5 · FROM MAN TO MAN

1. Peter L. Berger's *The Noise of Solemn Assemblies* is one long indictment of the Church for this failure. Note his description of religion in America as "a starry-eyed optimism, a naïve credulity in the ideologies of the *status quo*, something that goes well together with an unthinking if benign conservatism in all areas of life" (p. 13). Cf. Pierre Berton, *The Comfortable Pew*, pp. 36 ff. Myrdal, speaking of the silence of churches, says that "The average Southern white man, for natural reasons, can only be gratified not to have his stand on race relations exposed to the teachings of Christianity" (*An American Dilemma*, p. 869). But this is not new. Yinger, in *Religion, Society and the Individual*, says that "In the United States, by the latter half of the nineteenth century, there was scarcely a doubt in the established Protestant churches that the 'Gilded Age' was solving most of man's problems, that the economic theories of the middle and

upper classes were religiously valid—and that those who opposed the prevailing distribution of power and wealth, therefore, were anti-Christian" (p. 218). In the same period "Powderly, head of the knights of Labor, made the statement that if the Sermon on the Mount were preached without reference to its author, the preacher would be warned not to repeat such utopian ravings" (pp. 220 f.).

2. Along with pessimism about the Church, there is also the naïve optimism about the world, so bitingly described by Dan Wakefield in "Slick-paper Christianity" (reprinted in Stein, Vidich, and Manning, eds., *Identity and Anxiety* pp. 410–415). Note, for example, his remark that "It's a peculiar reassurance that popular Christianity seeks to convey to its followers—that its current disciples are so like the man in the street, and so unlike the Savior of the Bible" (p. 414). Or, again, "Maybe that's why the current religious revival in America is such a hollow pretense, and why it has had so little regenerating effect on the moral temper of the times. Too many religious leaders have sought to be "together" with their era and become shabby followers and imitators rather than leaders. In the desperate effort to be up-to-date, they have dressed Jesus Christ in a grey flannel suit and smothered his spirit in the folds of conformity" (p. 415).

3. Bonhoeffer and others argue that technologically oriented man no longer feels the need for the kind of explanation of life and the universe provided by the Bible; science provides by itself adequate explanations and mastery: "The technical science of the modern western world has emancipated itself from any kind of subservience. It is in essence not service but mastery. . . . Technology has become an end in itself" (*Ethics*, pp. 34 f.).

4. There is, of course, always the danger of such a program becoming a course in "How to be a successful Christian," which may really mean "How to use God in order to be a success." Many success-oriented business and professional people are no doubt attracted to such a movement for precisely these reasons, but this can never be the goal of any genuinely Christian movement. The Christian does not use God, but is used by Him.

5. It is because of this kind of pragmatic thinking that Loukes, in *Teenage Religion* (a study of the Religious Instruction Program in British secondary schools) argues for a problem-oriented approach rather than a subject-matter-oriented approach. The Bible, he argues, must be relevant to felt needs (p. 8).

6. On the dangers of clerical professionalism, Munby has said, "The clergy as professionals have no experience of other spheres of life. . . . They are tempted to believe that when they have spoken the words of the Bible or the Prayer Book or the text-books of theology, they have preached the Gospel, and that it is the business of the world to learn these words. They are tempted to believe that being a Christian means participating in the activities in which clergy are active, and that the 'world' against which the Church is set consists of all those activities in which the clergy do not participate" (*The Idea of a Secular Society*, p. 66). The effect of this psychological isolationism on communication is, of course, disastrous.

7. Cf. G. Ernest Wright and Reginald H. Fuller, *The Book of the Acts of God*.

8. No doubt a part of such criticism comes from the formalistic attitude scored by Berton: "Though the Sabbath and the Church were made for man and not man for the Sabbath, most ministers continue to affirm that you cannot be a good Christian unless you attend Church regularly. When the Church gets involved, as it occasionally does, with the mass media, this is the essence of its advertising message. 'Attend the Church of your choice' is the slogan and not 'love one another'" (*op. cit.*, p. 71).

9. Cf. Harvey Cox's argument that "Men must be called away from their fascination with other worlds—astrological, metaphysical, or religious—and summoned to confront the concrete issues of this one, 'wherein alone the true call of God can be found'" (*The Secular City*, p. 154). The need to live a Christian life in the here and now, with all its problems and agonizing ambiguities, is a leitmotiv of Bonhoeffer in the two books written in prison, *Prisoner for God* and *Ethics*.

10. This restructuring, together with the previous problems mentioned (selectivity and skewing), is no doubt largely responsible for what Jensen in *Myth and Cult Among Primitive Peoples* calls the "semantic depletion" of myth in the process of successive transmissions from person to person. Jensen considers this depletion to be universal and inevitable in the history of religious ideas. Cf. also John Gillin, "Personality formation from the comparative cultural point of view" (in Kluckhohn and Murray, eds., *Personality in Nature, Society, and Culture*, pp. 164–175). He cites Bartlett and Nadel, who "have shown by experiments on different African tribes that the cultural patterns have a strong influence

on the restructuralization of memories. . . . For example, if an individual is asked to repeat a European story, he always tends to cast it with characters typical of his tribal folklore and to repeat it in a pattern of sequence and with twists of plot characteristic of the native stories" (p. 167).

## 6. FROM GOD TO MAN

1. It is also true, as Berton has said, that many Christians have reduced their faith to esoteric mysteries "too difficult to be understood by the masses" (*The Comfortable Pew*, p. 90).

2. Cf. Bultmann's statement that *"Theological propositions—*even those of the New Testament—can never be the *object* of faith, they can only be the *explication* of the understanding which is inherent in faith itself" (*Theology of the New Testament*, Vol. II, pp. 237 ff.).

3. Various writers have described the effects of this value grid; most assign an important role to language and/or culture in the process by which the grid becomes internalized in the individual. Kluckhohn and Murray, for example, say that "culture directs and often distorts man's perceptions of the external world. What effects social suggestion may have in setting frames of reference for perception have been shown experimentally. Culture acts as a set of blinders, or series of lenses, through which men view their environments" ("Personality formation: the determinants," in Kluckhohn and Murray, eds. *Personality in Nature, Society, and Culture*, p. 45). Obviously, one of the most important aspects of this grid is that it determines what the individual will consider to be important or trivial, good or bad, etc. In other words, it determines values.

4. In discussing the religious dimensions of the human ego it is important to distinguish two quite different meanings: (1) the ego as the aggressive, self-centered, and rebellious component of personality, i.e., the element in man which revolts against the will and purpose of God, and (2) the ego as the integrating element of human personality. It is this first meaning of ego to which we refer in this section, for it is this rebellious part of man which must be "captured and brought under control." The other aspect of the ego remains as a dynamic component in the "new man."

5. In claiming this essential weakness of irresponsible dictators, we do not overlook or underestimate the terrifying effects of overwhelming power to do evil. It is only in the long view of history that the essential weakness manifests itself and demonstrates the thesis that real strength lies in the willing adherence of free men rather than in the forced obedience of slaves.

6. See again Dan Wakefield, "Slick-paper Christianity": "Blessed are the stable-in-heart, kids, for they will see good weekly pay checks" (p. 413).

7. Cf. Berger's argument that a true understanding of Christian faith leads, not to adjustment to and integration into culture, but to alienation (*The Noise of Solemn Assemblies*, pp. 119 f., 133).

# Index

*Format by Margaret F. Plympton*
*Set in Linotype Electra*
*Composed by The Haddon Craftsmen, Inc.*
*Printed by Murray Printing Company*
*Bound by The Haddon Craftsmen, Inc.*
HARPER & ROW, PUBLISHERS, INCORPORATED